FLASHMAPS
CHICAGO

Editor
Steven K. Amsterdam

Creative Director
Fabrizio La Rocca

Cartographer
David Lindroth

Designer
Tigist Getachew

Editorial Contributors
Helayne Schiff
Martha Schulman

Cartographic Contributors
Edward Faherty
Tim Faherty
Page Lindroth
Dan Neumann
Eric Rudolph

ESSENTIAL INFORMATION — MAP

Important Telephone Numbers	iv–v
Northeast Illinois	1
Chicagoland	2
Chicago	3
Streetfinder/Downtown	4
Streetfinder/North Side	5
Zip Codes	6
Neighborhoods	7
Hospitals & 24-Hour Pharmacies	8
McCormick Place	9
Consulates	10
Libraries	11
Universities, Colleges & Schools	12
University of Chicago	13
Illinois Institute of Technology	14
Northwestern University	15

TRANSPORTATION — MAP

Midway Airport	16
O'Hare International Airport	17
Buses/Near North	18
Buses/Downtown & Loop	19
CTA/Area	20
CTA/Near North	21
CTA/Downtown & Loop	22
Metra/ Northern Suburbs	23
Metra/ Western & Southern Suburbs	24
Driving & Parking	25

EXPLORING — MAP

Top Attractions	26
Architecture	27
Oak Park	28
Hyde Park & Kenwood	29
Evanston	30
Skokie	31
Bronzetown	32
Churches, Temples & Mosques	33
Museums	34
John G Shedd Aquarium	35

EXPLORING (cont.)   MAP

Art Institute of Chicago	36
Field Museum	37
Museum of Science and Industry	38
Art Galleries	39

PARKS & RECREATION   MAP

Beaches	40
Parks	41
Lincoln Park	42
Lincoln Park Zoo	43
Stadiums & Arenas	44
Public Golf Courses	45

SHOPPING   MAP

Shopping/Near North & Loop	46
Shopping/North Side	47

DINING & LODGING   MAP

Restaurants/Downtown	48
Restaurants/Near North	49
Restaurants/North Side, Bucktown & Wicker Park	50
Restaurants/South Side	51
Hotels/O'Hare Airport Area	52
Hotels/Greater Chicago	53

NIGHTLIFE   MAP

Performing Arts	54
Symphony Center	55
Movies	56
Nightlife/Near North & Downtown	57
Nightlife/North Side	58

Special Sales

Fodor's Travel Publications are available at special discounts for bulk purchases for sales promotions or premiums. Special editions, including personalized covers, excerpts of existing guides, and corporate imprints, can be created in large quantities for special needs. For more information, contact your local bookseller or write to Special Markets, Fodor's Travel Publications, 201 East 50th St., New York, NY 10022. Inquiries from Canada should be directed to your local Canadian bookseller or sent to Random House of Canada, Ltd., Marketing Dept., 2775 Matheson Blvd. East, Mississauga, Ontario L4W4P7. Inquiries from the United Kingdom should be sent to Fodor's Travel Publications, 20 Vauxhall Bridge Rd., London, England SW1V 2SA. **ISBN 0-679-00240-5**

PRINTED IN THE UNITED STATES OF AMERICA 10 9 8 7 6 5 4 3 2 1

Area Codes: All (312) unless otherwise noted.

EMERGENCIES

Abducted, Abused and Exploited Children
☎ 800/248-8020

Ambulance/ Fire/Police ☎ 911

Illinois AIDS/STD Hotline
☎ 800/243-2437

Illinois Poison Center
☎ 800/942-5969

Medical Referral Service
☎ 670-2550

National Runaway Switchboard
☎ 800/621-4000

Travelers Aid ☎ 773/894-2427

Walgreens 24-hour Pharmacy
☎ 800/925-4733

Youth Crisis Hotline
☎ 800/448-4663

SERVICES

AAA ☎ 800/222-4357

Alcoholics Anonymous
☎ 312/346-1475

Chicago Convention and Tourism Bureau ☎ 800/226-6632

Chicago Office of Tourism
☎ 744-2400

Chicago Sun-Times Infoline
☎ 321-2211

Consumer Protection
☎ 312/814-3580

Consumer Services ☎ 312/744-9400

Cook County Commission on Human Rights ☎ 312/603-1100

Gay and Lesbian Helpline
☎ 773/929-4357

Gay and Lesbian Anti-Violence Project ☎ 773/871-2273

Mayor's Office for People with Disabilities ☎ 744-6673

Mayor's Office of Special Events
☎ 744-3379

Police/Fire Non-Emergency
☎ 312/746-6000

Traffic Ticket Information
☎ 312/822-3604

U.S. Postal Service ☎ 800/275-8777

Weather Information
☎ 708/298-1413

TRANSPORTATION

American United Cab Co.
☎ 773/248-7600

Amtrak ☎ 800/872-7245

Checker Taxi ☎ 243-2537

Continental Airport Express
☎ 454-7799

CW Limousine Service
☎ 773/493-2700

Flash Cab ☎ 773/561-1444

O'Hare International Airport
☎ 773/686-2200

Greyhound ☎ 800/231-2222

Greyhound Bus Terminal
☎ 408-5970

Metra ☎ 322-6777

Midway Airport ☎ 773/838-0600

RTA Travel Information ☎ 836-7000

Yellow Cab Co. ☎ 829-4222

ENTERTAINMENT

Chicago Classical Music Alliance
☎ 987-9296

Chicago Live Concert Hotline
☎ 666-6667

Chicago Symphony Orchestra
☎ 294-3000

Civic Orchestra ☎ 294-3420

Dance Hotline ☎ 419-8383

Hot Tix ☎ 977-1755

Jazz Hotline ☎ 427-3300

Lyric Opera ☎ 332-2244

Moviefone ☎ 444-FILM

Ticketmaster ☎ 559-8989,
☎ 902-1500 (Arts line)

PARKS AND RECREATION

Chicago Park District ☎ 747-2200

Chicago Park District Beach Info
☎ 747-0832

Chicago Park District Golf Info
☎ 245-0909

Chicago Sportfishing Association
☎ 922-1100

Chicagoland Bicycle Federation
☎ 427-3325

City of Chicago Fishing Hotline
☎ 744-3370

SPECTATOR SPORTS

Chicago Bears ☎ 847/615-BEAR

Chicago Blackhawks Tickets
☎ 455-7000

Chicago Bulls Tickets ☎ 455-4000

Chicago Cubs Tickets
☎ 773/404-2827

Chicago Fire Tickets
☎ 888/657-3473

Chicago White Sox Tickets
☎ 674-1000

Northwestern Wildcats Tickets
☎ 847/491-2287

United Center ☎ 455-4500

TOURS

Walking Tours:

Chicago Architecture Foundation
☎ 922-3432

Chicago Neighborhood Tours
☎ 742-1190

**Chicago Sun-Times Operations
Tours** ☎ 321-3268

Chicago Supernatural Tours
☎ 708/499-0300

**Frank Lloyd Wright Home and
Studio Foundation of Oak Park**
☎ 708/848-1976

Friends of the Chicago River
☎ 939-0490

Boat Tours:

**Chicago Architecture Foundation
River Cruise** ☎ 922-3432

Mercury Chicago Skyline Cruiseline
☎ 332-1353

Shoreline Marine ☎ 222-9328

Wendella Sightseeing Boats
☎ 337-1446

Bus Tours:

American Sightseeing ☎ 251-3100

Black CouTours ☎ 773/233-8907

Chicago Motor Coach Co.
☎ 666-1000

Chicago Trolley Company
☎ 663-0260

Tour Black Chicago ☎ 332-2323

32

Winthrop Harbor

131 173
Zion

Beach
Park

131 Waukegan

North Chicago

Lake Bluff

41 Lake Forest

43

22 Highwood
Bannockburn
Deerfield   Highland
41   Park
94
68
94 Glencoe
Northbrook
43
Winnetka
21   Kenilworth
294 58   Wilmette
14
94 Skokie 58 Evanston

43 14

90 72   14
41
90
94   19

50
64

Oak Park   41

43
290
Cicero   38
Berwyn
20 34   55
            90
            94 41
CHICAGO
Midway
Airport

171
Burbank 50   90
294   94
43
45   12 12
            20 20
COOK COUNTY
Palos   57
Park   83
        Palos   94
50   Heights Blue
Orland 294   Island
7
Orland 43   Dolton   East
Park   Chicago
Oak Forest 57   South 41
Orland 6   Holland 20 312 912
Hills   Markham   6   90
Tinley   80   152
Park   57   294 Lansing 6 Hammond Gary
80   Hazel Thornton 394   80 53
Frankfort 57 Crest Glenwood   94
45 50   Flossmoor 1 Chicago Munster
            Matteson   Heights Highland 55 65

Lake Michigan

0   4 miles
0   6 km

N

INDIANA
ILLINOIS

12

12 20

12

90
80 6
94 51
6
65
51

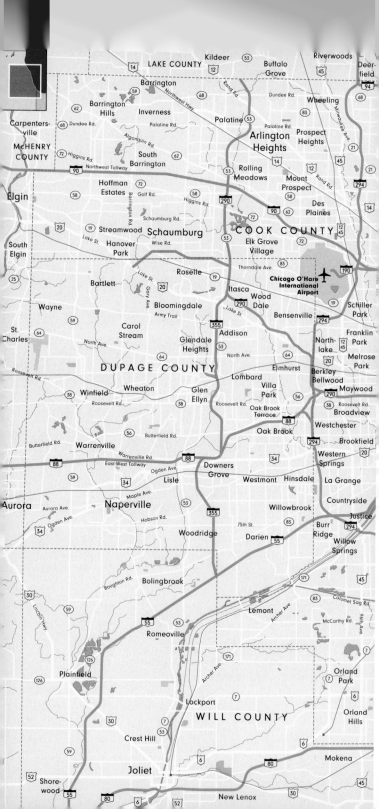

Letter codes refer to grid sectors on preceding map

NORTH-SOUTH STREETS
(**N** prefix north of Madison;
S prefix south of Madison)
Aberdeen St A2, A3
Archer Ave A6, B5
Astor St B1
Blue Island Ave A5
Branch St A1, A2
Calumet Ave C5, C6
Cambridge Ave A2
Canal Port A6, B5
Canal St B3, B6
Carpenter St A2, A6
Cherry Ave A1
Clark St B1, B6
Cleveland Ave B1, B2
Clybourn Ave A1, B1
Columbus Ave C3, C5
Cottage Grove Ave C6
Crosby St A1, A2
Dan Ryan Expwy A2, B6
Dearborn St B1, B6
Desplaines St A2, A6
Dewitt Pl C2
Fairbanks Ct C2, C3
Federal St B4, B6
Field Blvd C3
Franklin St B1, B4
Garland St C1
Green St A2, A4
Halsted St A1, A6
Hickory Ave A1, A2
Hooker St A1, A2
Hudson Ave B1, B2
Indiana Ave C5, C6
Jefferson St A3, A5
JFK Expwy A2
Kingsbury St A1, B3
Lake Shore Dr C1, C6
Larrabee St. A1, A2
LaSalle St B1, B4
Lumber St A6, B5
McClurg Ct C2, C3
Michigan Ave C2, C6
Miller St A4
Milwaukee Ave A2, B3
ML King Jr Dr C6
Mohawk St A1
Newbury St A5
Ogden Ave A2, B1
Orleans St B1, B3
Park Ave B1
Peoria St A2, A6
Plymouth St B4
Prairie Ave C5, C6
Princeton Ave B6
Rush St B1, C2
Sangamon St A2, A6
Sedgewick St B1, B2

Silverton Way C6
St Clair St C2
State Pkwy B1
State St B1, B6
Stetson Ave C3
Stevenson Expwy A6, C6
Stewart Ave B6
Union Ave A2, A6
Wabash Ave B2, B6
Wacker Dr B4, C3
Wells St B1, B5
Wentworth Ave B6

EAST-WEST STREETS
(**W** prefix west of State St;
E prefix east of State St)
11th St B4, C4
12th St A5
13th St A5, C5
14th Pl A5, B5
14th St A5, C5
16th St A5, C5
17th St A5, B5
18th Pl A5
18th St A5, C5
19th St A5, B5
21st St A6, C6
22nd Pl B6
23rd Pl B6, C6
23rd St B6, C6
24th Pl B6
24th St B6, C6
25th Pl B6
25th St A6, C6
26th St A6, C6
8th St B4, C4
9th St B4, C4
Adams St A3, C3
Alexander St B6
Balbo Dr B4, C4
Banks St B1
Barber St A5
Bellevue St B1, C1
Blackhawk St A1, B1
Burton Pl B1
Carroll Ave A3
Cedar St B1, C1
Cermak Rd. A6, C6
Chestnut St A2, C2
Chicago Ave A2, C2
Congress Pkwy B4, C4
Couch Pl B3
Court Pl B3
Cullerton St A6, C6
Delaware St B2, C2
Depot St A5, B5
Division St A1, C1
Eastman Ave A1

Eisenhower Expwy A4, B4
Elm St A1, C1
Erie St A2, C2
Evergreen Ave A1
Fry St A2
Fulton St A3, B3
Goethe St B1, C1
Grand Ave A2, C2
Haddock Pl B3, C3
Harrison Ave A4, C4
Hill St B1
Hobbie St A1
Hubbard St A2, C3
Huron St A2, C2
Institute Pl B2
Jackson Blvd A4, C4
Jackson Dr C4
Kinzie St A3, C3
Lake St A3, C3
Liberty St A5
Locust St B2
Madison St A3, C3
Maple St B1
Marble Pl B3
Maxwell St A5, B5
McFetridge Dr C5
Monroe Dr C3
Monroe St A3, C3
N Water St C3
North Ave A1, B1
North Blvd B1
O'Brien St A5
Oak St A2, C2
Ohio St A2, C2
Ontario St B2, C2
Pearson St B2, C2
Polk St A4, B4
Randolph St A3, C3
Roosevelt Rd A5, C5
S Water St C3
Schiller St B1
Scott St B1, C1
Solidarity Dr C5
Sullivan St B1
Superior St A2, C2
Taylor St A4, B4
Van Buren St A4, C4
Waldron Dr C5
Walton St B2, C2
Washington Blvd A3, C3
Weed St A1
Wendell St B1

Letter codes refer to grid sectors on preceding map

NORTH-SOUTH STREETS
(**N** prefix north of Madison)

Ashland Ave A1, A6
Beacon St B1, B2
Belmont Harbor Dr C3
Bissell St B5, B6
Bosworth Ave A2, A6
Broadway B1, C4
Burling St C4, C6
Cambridge Ave C4, C5
Cannon Dr C4, C5
Clarendon St B1, B3
Clark St A1, C6
Cleveland Ave C5, C6
Clifton Ave B2, B6
Clybourn Ave A4, B6
Commonwealth Ave C4, C5
Damen Ave A1, A6
Dayton St B2, B6
Dominick St A5, A6
Dover St A1, A2
Elaine Pl C3
Elston Ave A5,B6
Fremont St B3,B6
Geneva Ter C5
Glenwood Ave B1
Grant Pl C5
Greenview Ave A3, A6
Halsted Ave B3, B6
Hampden Ct C4, C5
Hazel St B2
Hermitage Ave A1, A6
Honore St A6
Howe St C6
Hudson Ave C5, C6
Janssen Ave A1, A5
Kenmore Ave B1, B6
Kingsbury St B6
Lake Shore Dr B1, C4
Lakeview Ave C4, C5
Lakewood Ave B3, B6
Larrabee St C5, C6
LaSalle St C6
Lincoln Ave A2, C6
Lincoln Park W C5, C6
Lister Ave A5
Magnolia Ave B1, B6
Malden St B1, B2
Marcey St B6
Marine Dr B1, C3
Marshfield Ave B3, B6
Maud Ave B6
Mendell St A6
Mildred Ave B4, B5
Mohawk St C6
Orchard St C4, C6
Orleans St C6
Park Ave C6

Paulina St A1, A6
Pine Grove Ave C3, C4
Racine Ave B1, B6
Ravenswood Ave A1, A4
Reta Ave B3
Sedgewick St C5, C6
Seminary Ave B3, B6
Sheffield Ave B3, B6
Sheridan Rd B1, C4
Simonds Dr C1
Surrey Ct B5
Throop St B6
Waterloo Ct C4
Wayne Ave B3, B5
Wells St C6
Wilton Ave B3, B5
Winchester Ave A1, A6
Winthrop Ave B1, B2
Wolcott Ave A1, A6
Wood St A6

EAST-WEST STREETS
(**W** prefix west of State)

Addison St A3, C3
Agatite Ave B2, C2
Ainslie St A1, B1
Aldine Ave B4, C4
Altgeld St A5, A5
Argyle St A1, B2
Arlington Pl C5
Armitage Ave A6, C6
Barry Ave A4, C4
Belden Ave A5, C5
Belle Plaine Ave A2, B2
Belmont Ave A4, C4
Bernice Ave A3
Berteau Ave A2
Bittersweet Pl C2
Bloomingdale Ave A6
Bradley Pl A3, B3
Briar Pl C4
Brompton Ave C3
Buckingham Pl B4, C4
Byron St A3, B3
Carmen Ave A1, B1
Castlewood Ter B1, C1
Concord Pl B6
Cornelia Ave A3, C3
Cortland St A6, B6
Cullom Ave A2, B2
Cuyler Ave A2, C2
Dakin St B3
Deming Pl C5
Dickens Ave A6, C6
Diversey Ave A4, C4
Drummond Pl C5
Eastwood Ave B1
Eddy St A3, B3
Eugene St. C6

Fletcher St A4, B4
Foster Ave A1, B1
Fullerton Ave A5, C5
George St A4, B4
Gordon Ter C2
Grace St A3, C3
Grant Pl C5
Gunnison St B1
Hawthorne Pl C3
Henderson St A4, B4
Hutchinson St A2, C2
Irving Park Rd A3, B3
Junior Ave B2
Kemper Pl C5
Lakeside Ave B1, C1
Larchmont Ave A3
Lawrence Ave A1, C1
Lawrence Dr C1
Leland Ave A1, C1
Lill Ave A5, B5
Margate Ter B1
Melrose St A4, C4
Menomonee St C6
Montana St A5, B5
Montrose Ave A2, C2
Montrose Dr C2
Nelson St A4, B4
Newport Ave A3, C3
North Ave A6, C6
Oakdale Ave A4, C4
Patterson St A3, C3
Pensacola Ave A2, C2
Roscoe St A3,C4
Roslyn Pl C5
School St A4, B4
Schubert Ave B5, C5
St James Pl C5
St Paul Ave A6, C6
Stratford Pl C3
Sunnyside Ave A2, B2
Surf St C4
Wabansia Ave A6
Waveland Ave A3, C3
Webster Ave A5, C5
Wellington Ave A4, C4
Willow St B6, C6
Wilson Ave A2, C2
Wilson Dr C2
Windsor Ave B2
Winnemac Ave A1, B1
Winona St A1, B1
Wisconsin St B6, C6
Wolfram St A4, B4
Wrightwood Ave A5, C5

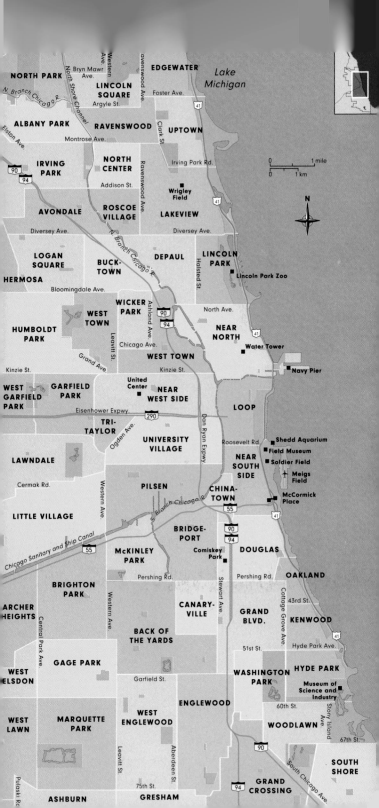

Listed by Site Number

1 Edgewater Medical Ctr

2 Swedish Covenant Hospital

3 Methodist Hospital of Chicago

4 Ravenswood Hospital Medical Ctr

5 Louis A Weiss Memorial Hospital

6 Thorek Hospital and Medical Center

7 Our Lady of Resurrection Medical Ctr

8 Walgreens

9 Illinois Masonic Medical Center

10 St Joseph Hospital

11 Columbus Hospital

12 Children's Memorial Hospital

13 Grant Hospital

14 Walgreens

15 St Elizabeth's Hospital

16 St Mary of Nazareth Hospital Center

17 Norwegian American Hospital

18 Walgreens

19 Northwestern Memorial Hospital

20 Walgreens

21 Rush-Presbyterian-St Luke's Medical Ctr

22 University of Illinois at Chicago Medical Center

23 Cook County Hospital

24 Bethany Hospital

25 St Anthony Hospital

26 Mercy Hospital and Medical Center

27 Michael Reese Hospital and Medical Center

28 Walgreens

29 University of Chicago Medical Center

30 Doctor's Hospital of Hyde Park

31 LaRabida Children's Hospital

32 Jackson Park Hospital and Medical Center

Listed Alphabetically

Bethany Hospital, 24.
3435 W Van Buren St
☎ 773/265-7700

Children's Memorial Hospital, 12.
707 W Fullerton Ave ☎ 773/880-4000

Columbus Hospital, 11.
2520 N Lakeview Ave
☎ 773/388-7300

Cook County Hospital, 23.
1835 W Harrison St ☎ 633-6000

Doctor's Hospital of Hyde Park, 30.
5800 S Stony Island Ave
☎ 773/643-9200

Edgewater Medical Center, 1.
5700 N Ashland Ave ☎ 773/878-6000

Grant Hospital, 13.
550 W Webster Ave ☎ 773/883-2000

Illinois Masonic Medical Center, 9.
836 W Wellington Ave
☎ 773/975-1600

Jackson Park Hospital and Medical Center, 32. 7531 S Stony Island Ave
☎ 773/947-7500

LaRabida Children's Hospital, 31.
65th St and Lake Michigan
☎ 773/363-6700

Louis A Weiss Memorial Hospital, 5. 4646 N Marine Dr ☎ 773/878-8700

Mercy Hospital and Medical Center , 26. 2525 S Michigan Ave
☎ 567-2000

Methodist Hospital of Chicago, 3.
5025 N Paulina St ☎ 773/271-9040

Michael Reese Hospital and Medical Center, 27. 2929 S Ellis Ave
☎ 791-2000

Northwestern Memorial Hospital, 19. 250 E Superior St ☎ 908-2000

Norwegian American Hospital, 17.
1044 N Francisco Ave
☎ 773/292-8200

Our Lady of Resurrection Medical Center, 7. 5645 W Addison St
☎ 773/282-7000

Ravenswood Hospital Medical Center, 4. 4550 N Winchester Ave
☎ 773/878-4300

Rush-Presbyterian-St Luke's Medical Center, 21.
1653 W Congress Pkwy ☎ 942-5000

St Anthony Hospital, 25.
2875 W 19th St ☎ 773/521-1710

St Elizabeth's Hospital, 15.
1431 N Claremont Ave
☎ 773/278-2000

St Joseph Hospital, 10.
2900 N Lake Shore Dr
☎ 773/665-3086

St Mary of Nazareth Hospital Center, 16. 2233 W Division St
☎ 770-2000

Swedish Covenant Hospital, 2.
5145 N California Ave
☎ 773/878-8200

Thorek Hospital and Medical Center, 6. 850 W Irving Park Rd
☎ 773/525-6780

University of Chicago Medical Center, 29. 5841 S Maryland Ave
☎ 773/702-1000

University of Illinois at Chicago Medical Center, 22.
1740 W Taylor St ☎ 996-7000

24-HOUR PHARMACIES

Walgreens, 8.
Broadway & Belmont Ave
☎ 773/327-3591

Walgreens, 14. 1601 N Wells St
☎ 642-4008

Walgreens, 18. 757 N Michigan Ave
☎ 664-8686

Walgreens, 28. 1554 E 55th St
☎ 773/667-1177

Walgreens, 20. 641 N Clark St
☎ 587-1416

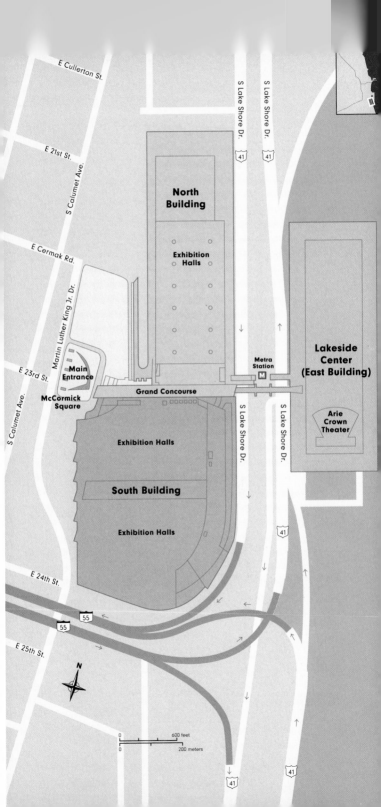

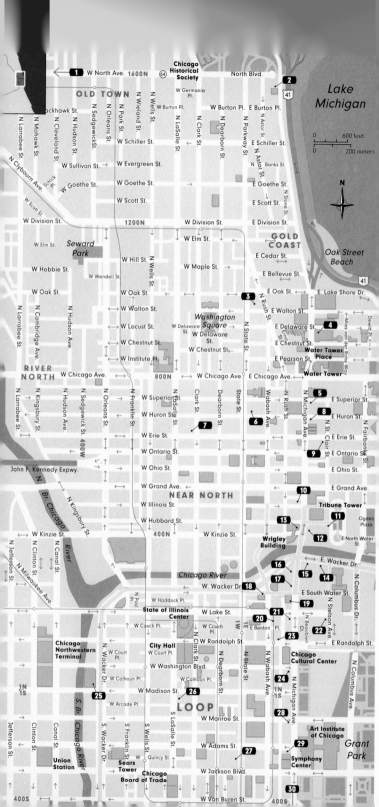

Listed by Site Number

1 Dominican Republic	**10** Italy	**22** Canada
2 Poland	**11** India	**23** Indonesia
3 Portugal	**12** Brazil	**24** Philippines
4 Chile	**13** Austria	**25** Venezuela
4 Denmark	**13** Great Britian	**26** Ghana
5 France	**14** Israel	**27** Haiti
5 Switzerland	**15** Belgium	**28** El Salvador
6 Ukraine	**16** Turkey	**29** South Africa
7 China	**17** Mexico	**30** Liberia
8 Germany	**18** Thailand	
9 Greece	**19** Guatemala	
10 Columbia	**20** Costa Rica	
10 Ecuador	**21** Peru	
	21 Spain	

Listed Alphabetically

Austria, 13. 400 N Michigan Ave ☎ 222-1515

Belgium, 15. 333 N Michigan Ave ☎ 263-6624

Brazil, 12. 401 N Michigan Ave ☎ 464-0244

Canada, 22. 180 N Stetson Ave ☎ 616-1860

Chile, 4. 875 N Michigan Ave ☎ 654-8780

China, 7. 100 W Erie St ☎ 573-3070

Colombia, 10. 500 N Michigan Ave ☎ 923-1196

Costa Rica, 20. 185 N Wabash Ave ☎ 263-2772

Denmark, 4. 875 N Michigan Ave ☎ 787-8780

Dominican Republic, 1. 3228 W North Ave ☎ 773/772-6363

Ecuador, 10. 500 N Michigan Ave ☎ 329-0266

El Salvador, 28. 104 S Michigan Ave ☎ 332-1393

France, 5. 737 N Michigan Ave ☎ 787-5359

Germany, 8. 676 N Michigan Ave ☎ 580-1199

Ghana, 26. 19 S LaSalle St ☎ 236-0440

Great Britian, 13. 400 N Michigan Ave ☎ 464-5120

Greece, 9. 650 N St Clair Ave ☎ 335-3915

Guatemala, 19. 230 N Michigan Ave ☎ 332-1587

Haiti, 27. 220 S State St ☎ 922-4004

India, 11. 455 N City Front Plaza Dr ☎ 595-0405

Indonesia, 23. 72 E Randolph St ☎ 345-9300

Israel, 14. 111 E Wacker Dr ☎ 565-3300

Italy, 10. 500 N Michigan Ave ☎ 467-1550

Liberia, 30. 2230 E 71st St ☎ 773/643-8635

Mexico, 17. 300 N Michigan Ave ☎ 855-1380

Peru, 21. 180 N Michigan Ave ☎ 782-1599

Philippines, 24. 30 N Michigan Ave ☎ 332-6458

Poland, 2. 1530 N Lake Shore Dr ☎ 337-8166

Portugal, 3. 1955 N New England Ave ☎ 773/889-7405

South Africa, 29. 200 S Michigan Ave ☎ 939-7929

Spain, 21. 180 N Michigan Ave ☎ 782-4588

Switzerland, 5. 737 N Michigan Ave ☎ 915-0061

Thailand, 18. 35 E Wacker Dr ☎ 236-2447

Turkey, 16. 360 N Michigan Ave ☎ 263-0644

Ukraine, 6. 10 E Huron St ☎ 642-4388

Venezuela, 25. 20 N Wacker Dr ☎ 236-9655

Listed by Site Number

1 Edgewater
2 Albany Park
3 Bezazian
4 Mayfair
5 Independence
6 Sulzer Regional
7 Uptown
8 Gerber/Hart Library
9 Hamlin Park
10 Merlo
11 Lincoln Park
12 Logan Square
13 Humboldt Park
14 Damen Avenue
15 Chicago Historical Society
16 West Town
17 Near North
18 Newberry Library
19 Instituto Cervantes
20 Moody Bible Institute
21 Eckhart Park
22 Midwest
23 Goethe-Institut

Chicago
24 Adler School of Professional Psychology
25 Mabel Manning
26 Chicago-Kent College of Law
27 Donors Forum of Chicago
28 Chicago Board of Trade
29 DePaul University Law Library
30 Harold Washington Library Center
31 Harrington Institute of Interior Design
32 Asher Library
33 Illinois Regional Library for the Blind and Physically Handicapped
33 Roosevelt
34 Rudy Lozano
35 Chinatown
36 McKinley Park

37 Richard J. Daley
38 Martin Luther King, Jr
39 Chicago Bee
40 Canaryville
41 Back of the Yards
42 Hall
43 Blackstone
44 Sherman Park
45 Lithuanian Research and Studies Center
46 John Crerar Science Library
47 National Opinion Research Center Library
48 South Shore
49 Woodson Regional

Listed Alphabetically

PUBLIC

Albany Park, 2. 5150 N Kimball Ave ☎ 744-1933

Back of the Yards, 41. 1743 W 47th St ☎ 747-8367

Bezazian, 3. 1226 W Ainslie St ☎ 744-0019

Blackstone, 43. 4904 S Lake Park Ave ☎ 747-0511

Canaryville, 40. 642 W 43rd St ☎ 747-0644

Chicago Bee, 39. 3647 S State St ☎ 747-6872

Chinatown, 35. 2353 S Wentworth Ave ☎ 747-8013

Damen Avenue, 14. 2056 N Damen Ave ☎ 744-6022

Eckhart Park, 21. 1371 W Chicago Ave ☎ 746-6069

Edgewater, 1. 1210 W Elmdale Ave ☎ 744-0718

Hall, 42. 4801 S Michigan Ave ☎ 747-2541

Hamlin Park, 9. 2205 W Belmont Ave ☎ 744-0166

Harold Washington Library Center, 30. 400 S State St ☎ 747-4300

Humboldt Park, 13. 1605 N Troy St. ☎ 744-2244

Illinois Regional Library for the Blind and Physically Handicapped, 33. 1055 W Roosevelt Rd ☎ 746-9210

Independence, 5. 3548 W Irving Park Rd ☎ 744-0900

Lincoln Park, 11. 1150 W. Fullerton Ave ☎ 744-1926

Logan Square, 12. 3255 W Altgeld St ☎ 744-5295

Mabel Manning, 25. 6 S Hoyne Ave ☎ 746-6800

Martin Luther King, Jr, 38. 3436 S King Dr ☎ 747-7543

Mayfair, 4. 4400 W Lawrence Ave ☎ 744-1254

McKinley Park, 36. 1915 W 35th Rd ☎ 747-6082

Merlo, 10. 644 W Belmont Ave ☎ 744-1139

Midwest, 22. 2335 W Chicago Ave ☎ 744-7788

Listed Alphabetically

Near North, 17.
310 W Division St ☎ 744-0991

Richard J. Daley, 37.
3400 S Halsted St ☎ 747-8990

Roosevelt, 33. 1055 W Roosevelt Rd
☎ 746-5656

Rudy Lozano, 34. 1805 S Loomis St
☎ 746-4329

Sherman Park, 44.
5440 S Racine Ave ☎ 747-0477

South Shore, 48. 2505 E 73rd St
☎ 747-5281

Sulzer Regional, 6.
4455 N Lincoln Ave ☎ 744-7616

Uptown, 7. 929 W Buena Ave
☎ 744-8400

West Town, 16. 1271 N Milwaukee Ave
☎ 744-1473

Woodson Regional, 49.
9525 S. Halsted St ☎ 747-6900

PROFESSIONAL

**Adler School of Professional
Psychology Library, 24.**
65 E Wacker Pl ☎ 201-5900

**Asher Library at Spertus Institute of
Jewish Studies, 32.**
618 S Michigan Ave ☎ 922-8248

**Chicago Board of Trade Library,
28.** 141 W Jackson Blvd ☎ 435-3552

Chicago Historical Society, 15.
1601 N. Clark St ☎ 642-4600

**Chicago-Kent College of Law
Library, 26.** 565 W Adams St
☎ 905-5600

DePaul University Law Library, 29.
25 E Jackson Blvd ☎ 362-8121

Donors Forum of Chicago, 27.
208 S LaSalle St ☎ 578-0090

Gerber/Hart Library, 8.
3352 N Paulina St ☎ 773/883-3003

Goethe-Institut Chicago, 23.
401 N Michigan Ave ☎ 329-0074

**Harrington Institute of Interior
Design Library, 31.**
410 S Michigan Ave ☎ 939-4975

Instituto Cervantes, 19.
875 N Michigan Ave ☎ 335-1996

John Crerar Science Library, 46.
5730 S Ellis Ave ☎ 773/702-7715

**Lithuanian Research and Studies
Center, 45.** 5620 S Claremont Ave
☎ 773/434-4545

Moody Bible Institute Library, 20.
820 N LaSalle ☎ 329-4136

**National Opinion Research Center
Library, 47.** 1155 E 60th St
☎ 773/753-7000

Newberry Library, 18.
60 W Walton St ☎ 943-9090

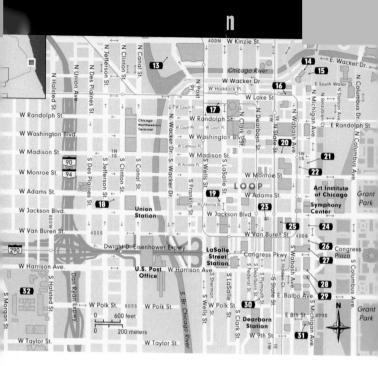

Listed by Site Number

1 Loyola University

2 Northeastern Illinois University

3 North Park University

4 Truman College

5 Wright College

6 Chicago National College of Naprapathy

7 Chicago School of Massage Therapy

8 DePaul University

9 Cooking and Hospitality Institute of Chicago

10 Scholl College of Podiatric Medicine

11 Loyola University

12 Northwestern University

13 Illinois Institute of Art

14 Adler School of Professional Psychology

15 Aurora University

16 Harold Washington College

17 Robert Morris College

18 Chicago-Kent College of Law

19 Lake Forest Graduate School of Management

20 International Academy of Merchandising and Design

21 National-Louis University

22 School of the Art Institute of Chicago

23 John Marshall Law School

24 American Academy of Art

25 DePaul University

26 Harrington Institute of Interior Design

27 Roosevelt University

28 Columbia College

29 Spertus Institute of Jewish Studies

30 Chicago School of Professional Psychology

31 East-West University

32 University of Illinois at Chicago

33 Malcolm X College

34 Rush University Chicago

35 West Side Technical Institute

36 Illinois Institute of Technology

37 Illinois College of Optometry

38 Lutheran School of Theology

39 McCormick Theological Seminary

40 Chicago Theological Seminary

41 University of Chicago

42 Chicago State University

43 Olive-Harvey College

44 Kennedy-King College

45 Richard J Daley College

Listed Alphabetically

Adler School of Professional Psychology, 14. 65 E Wacker Pl
☎ 201–5900

American Academy of Art, 24. 332 S Michigan Ave ☎ 461–0600

Aurora University, 15. 300 N Michigan Ave ☎ 357–1080

Chicago-Kent College of Law, 18. 565 W Adams St ☎ 906–5000

Chicago National College of Naprapathy, 6. 3330 N Milwaukee Ave ☎ 773/282–2686

Chicago School of Massage Therapy, 7. 2918 N Lincoln Ave ☎ 773/477–9444

Chicago School of Professional Psychology, 30. 806 S Plymouth Ct ☎ 786–9443

Chicago State University, 42. 9501 S Martin Luther King Dr ☎ 773/995–2000

Chicago Theological Seminary, 40. 5757 S University Ave ☎ 773/752–5757

Columbia College, 28. 600 S Michigan Ave ☎ 663–1600

Cooking and Hospitality Institute of Chicago, 9. 361 W Chestnut St ☎ 944–2725

DePaul University, 25. 1 E Jackson Blvd ☎ 362–8000

DePaul University, 8. 2320 N Kenmore Ave ☎ 362–8000

East-West University, 31. 816 S Michigan Ave ☎ 939–0111

Harold Washington College, 16. 30 E Lake St ☎ 553–5600

Harrington Institute of Interior Design, 26. 410 S Michigan Ave ☎ 939–4975

Illinois College of Optometry, 37. 3241 S Michigan Ave ☎ 225–1700

Illinois Institute of Art, 13. 350 N Orleans St ☎ 280–3500

Illinois Institute of Technology, 36. 3300 S Federal St ☎ 567–3000

International Academy of Merchandising and Design, 20. 1 N State St ☎ 541–3910

John Marshall Law School, 23. 315 S Plymouth Ct ☎ 427–2737

Kennedy-King College, 44. 6800 S Wentworth Ave ☎ 773/602–5000

Lake Forest Graduate School of Management, 19. 230 S LaSalle St ☎ 435–5330

Loyola Unversity, 1. 6525 N Sheridan Ave ☎ 773/274–3000

Loyola Unversity, 11. Water Tower Campus 820 N Michigan Ave ☎ 915–6000

Lutheran School of Theology, 38. 1100 E 55th St ☎ 773/753–0700

Malcolm X College, 33. 1900 W Van Buren Ave ☎ 850–7000

McCormick Theological Seminary, 39. 5555 S Woodlawn Ave ☎ 773/947–6300

National-Louis University, 21. 18 S Michigan Ave ☎ 621–9650

North Park University, 3. 3225 W Foster Ave ☎ 773/244–6200

Northeastern Illinois University, 2. 5500 N St. Louis Ave ☎ 773/583–4050

Northwestern University, 12. Chicago Ave and N Lake Shore Dr ☎ 503–8659

Olive-Harvey College, 43. 10001 S Woodlawn Ave ☎ 773/291–6100

Richard J Daley College, 45. 7500 S Pulaski Rd ☎ 773/838–7500

Robert Morris College, 17. 180 N LaSalle St ☎ 836–4608

Roosevelt University, 27. 430 S Michigan Ave ☎ 341–3500

Rush University Chicago, 34. 600 S Paulina St ☎ 942–7100

Scholl College of Podiatric Medicine, 10. 1001 N Dearborn St ☎ 280–2880

School of the Art Institute of Chicago, 22. 37 S Wabash Ave ☎ 899–5219

Spertus Institute of Jewish Studies, 29. 618 S Michigan Ave ☎ 322–1769

Truman College, 4. 1145 W Wilson Ave ☎ 773/878–1700

University of Chicago, 41. 5801 S Ellis Ave ☎ 773/702–1234

University of Illinois at Chicago, 32. 1200 W Harrison St ☎ 996–7000

West Side Technical Institute, 35. 2800 S Western Ave ☎ 773/843–4500

Wright College, 5. 4300 N Narragansett Ave ☎ 773/777–7900

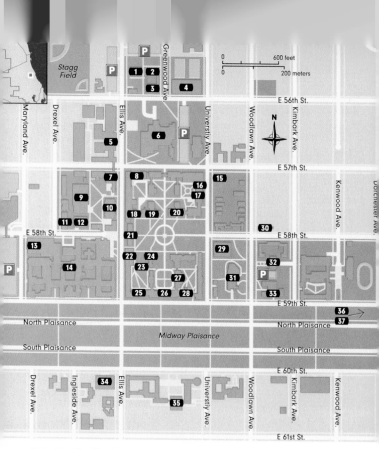

Listed by Site Number

1 Court Theatre

2 Cochrane-Woods Art Center

3 Smart Museum

4 Henry Crown Field House

5 Research Institutes

6 Regenstein Library

7 Kersten Physics Teaching Center

8 Snell-Hitchcock Halls

9 Crerar Library

10 Hinds Laboratory

11 Kovler Viral Oncology Laboratories

12 Cummings Life Science Center

13 Bernard Mitchell Hospital/Chicago Lying-in Hospital

14 University Hospitals

15 Quadrangle Club

16 Reynolds Club/University Theater

17 Mandel Hall

18 Jones Laboratory

19 Kent Chemical Laboratory

20 Ryerson Physical Laboratory

21 Administration Building

22 Cobb Hall

23 Bond Chapel

24 Swift Hall

25 Classics Building

26 Harper Memorial Library/College Admissions

27 Stuart Hall

28 Social Science Research

29 Oriental Institute

30 Robie House

31 Rockefeller Memorial Chapel

32 Woodward Court

33 Max Palevsky Cinema

34 Social Service Administration

35 Laird Bell Law Quadrangle/ D'Angelo Law Library

36 International House

37 Breckinridge House

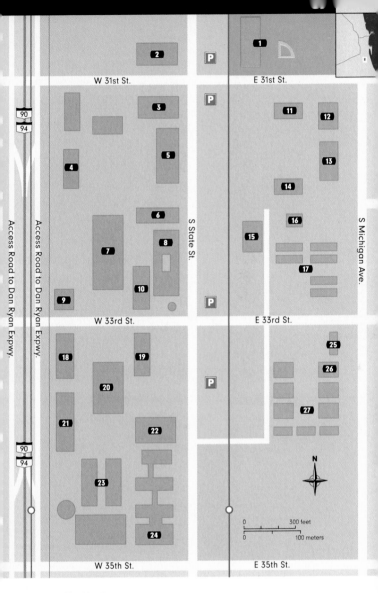

Listed by Site Number

1 Keating Sports Ctr	**10** Wishnick	**19** Siegel
2 Stuart	**11** Bailey Hall Apts	**20** Galvin Library
3 Life Sciences	**12** Cunningham Hall Apts	**21** IITRI Materials Research Building
4 VanderCook College of Music	**13** Gunsaulus Hall Apts	**22** Crown Hall
5 Eng 1 Building	**14** Carman Hall Apts	**23** IITRI Complex
6 Alumni Memorial Hall	**15** Commons Building	**24** IITRI Tower
7 Hermann Hall	**16** Chapel	**25** Farr Hall
8 Perlstein Hall	**17** Residence Hall Complex	**26** Res Hall Annex
9 Machinery Hall	**18** Main Building	**27** Fraternity Complex

Listed by Site Number

1	Student Residences	**12**	Norris University Ctr
2	Crown Sports Pavilion	**13**	McCormick Auditorium
3	Mudd Library	**14**	Pick-Steiger Concert Hall
4	Dearborn Observatory	**15**	Block Gallery
5	Garret Evangelical Theological Seminary	**16**	Theatre and Interpretation Ctr
6	Allen Center	**17**	Marjorie Ward Marshall Dance Ctr
7	Blomquist Recreation Center	**18**	Regenstein Hall of Music
8	Cresap Laboratory	**19**	Boathouse
9	Owen L Coon Forum	**20**	Chabad House
10	Deering Laboratory	**21**	Canterbury House
11	University Library		

22	Hillel Foundadtion
23	Kresge Centennial Hall
24	University Hall
26	Lutkin Hall
27	Music Administration
28	Rebecca Crown Center
29	Omni Orrington Hotel
30	Millar Chapel
31	Levere Memorial Temple
32	John Evans Alumni Center

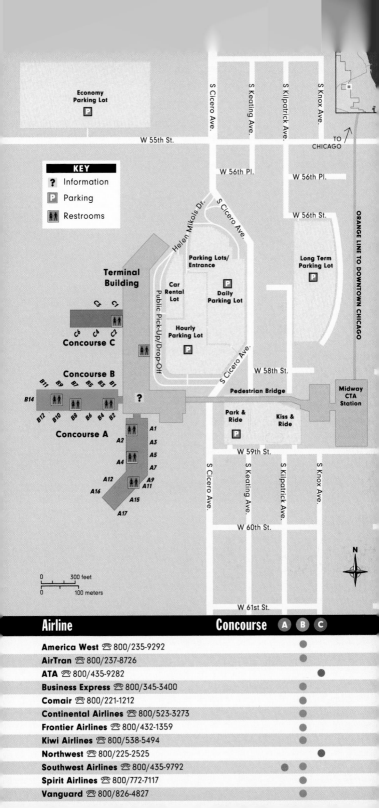

KEY
? Information
P Parking
👫 Restrooms

Economy Parking Lot P

W 55th St.

S Cicero Ave.
S Keating Ave.
S Kilpatrick Ave.
S Knox Ave.

TO CHICAGO

W 56th Pl.
W 56th Pl.
W 56th St.

ORANGE LINE TO DOWNTOWN CHICAGO

Helen Mikols Dr.
S Cicero Ave.

Parking Lots/ Entrance

Long Term Parking Lot P

Terminal Building

Car Rental Lot

Daily Parking Lot P

C3 C1

Public Pick-Up/Drop-Off

C6 C4 C2

Concourse C

Hourly Parking Lot P

Concourse B

B11 B9 B7 B5 B3 B1

B14
B12 B10 B8 B6 B4 B2

?

S Cicero Ave.
W 58th St.

Pedestrian Bridge

Midway CTA Station

Concourse A

A1
A2 A3
A4 A5
A7
A12 A9
A16 A11
A15
A17

Park & Ride P

Kiss & Ride

W 59th St.

S Cicero Ave.
S Keating Ave.
S Kilpatrick Ave.
S Knox Ave.

W 60th St.

N

0   300 feet
0   100 meters

W 61st St.

Airline	Concourse	A	B	C
America West ☎ 800/235-9292			●	
AirTran ☎ 800/237-8726			●	
ATA ☎ 800/435-9282				●
Business Express ☎ 800/345-3400			●	
Comair ☎ 800/221-1212			●	
Continental Airlines ☎ 800/523-3273			●	
Frontier Airlines ☎ 800/432-1359			●	
Kiwi Airlines ☎ 800/538-5494			●	
Northwest ☎ 800/225-2525				●
Southwest Airlines ☎ 800/435-9792		●	●	
Spirit Airlines ☎ 800/772-7117			●	
Vanguard ☎ 800/826-4827			●	

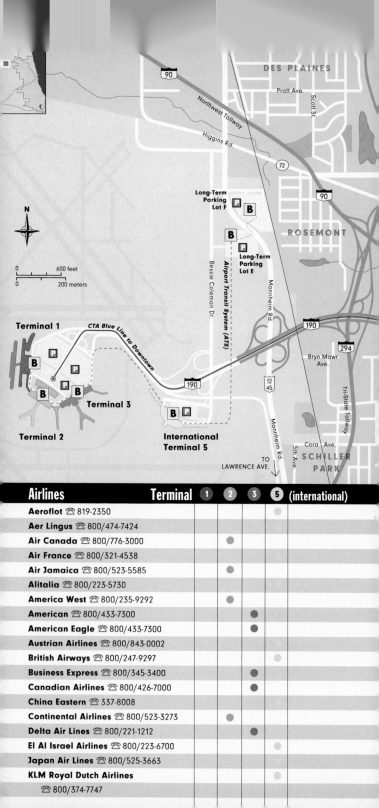

Airlines	Terminal 1	2	3	5 (international)
Aeroflot ☎ 819-2350				●
Aer Lingus ☎ 800/474-7424				
Air Canada ☎ 800/776-3000		●		
Air France ☎ 800/321-4538				
Air Jamaica ☎ 800/523-5585		●		
Alitalia ☎ 800/223-5730				
America West ☎ 800/235-9292		●		
American ☎ 800/433-7300			●	
American Eagle ☎ 800/433-7300			●	
Austrian Airlines ☎ 800/843-0002				
British Airways ☎ 800/247-9297				●
Business Express ☎ 800/345-3400			●	
Canadian Airlines ☎ 800/426-7000			●	
China Eastern ☎ 337-8008				
Continental Airlines ☎ 800/523-3273		●		
Delta Air Lines ☎ 800/221-1212			●	
El Al Israel Airlines ☎ 800/223-6700				●
Japan Air Lines ☎ 800/525-3663				
KLM Royal Dutch Airlines ☎ 800/374-7747				●

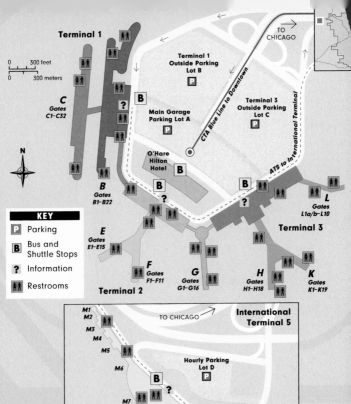

Airlines (cont.)	Terminal	1	2	3	5 (international)
Korean Air ☎ 800/438-5000					●
Kuwait Airways ☎ 800/458-9248					●
LOT Polish Airlines ☎ 800/223-0593					●
Lufthansa ☎ 800/645-3880		●			
Northwest Airlines ☎ 800/225-2525			●		●
Mexicana Airlines ☎ 800/531-7921					●
Reno Air ☎ 800/736-6247				●	
Quantas ☎ 800/227-4500					●
Sabena Belgium World Airlines					●
☎ 800/955-2000					
SAS ☎ 800/221-2350					●
Singapore Airlines ☎ 800/742-3333				●	
Swissair ☎ 800/221-4750					●
TWA ☎ 800/221-2000			●		
TAESA ☎ 800 328-2372					●
United ☎ 800/241-6522		●	●		
United Express ☎ 800/241-6522		●	●		
US Airways ☎ 800/428-4322			●		

CONTINUED ON MAP 19

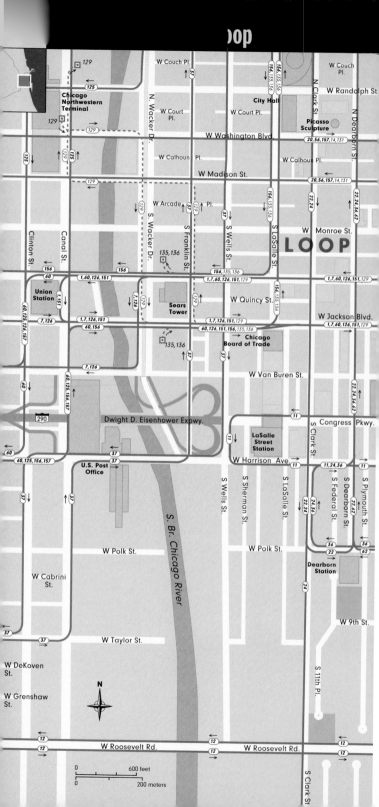

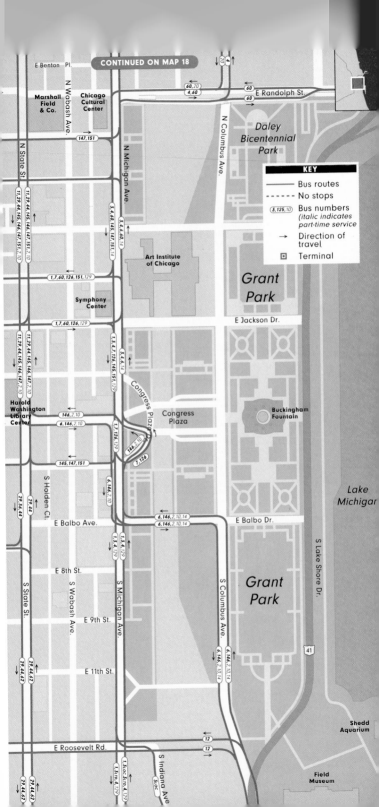

CONTINUED ON MAP 18

E Benton Pl.

N Wabash Ave.

Marshall Field & Co.

Chicago Cultural Center

147, 151

N State St.

N Michigan Ave.

11, 29, 44, 145, 146, 147, 151, 2, 10

11, 29, 44, 145, 146, 147, 151, 2, 10

3, 4, 60, 14

3, 4, 60, 145, 147, 151, 14

60, 20
4, 60

60

60

E Randolph St.

N Columbus Ave.

Daley Bicentennial Park

20

4

KEY

—— Bus routes

----- No stops

5, 125, 10 Bus numbers
(italic indicates part-time service)

→ Direction of travel

▫ Terminal

Art Institute of Chicago

Grant Park

1, 7, 60, 126, 151, 129

Symphony Center

1, 7, 60, 126, 129

E Jackson Dr.

1, 3, 4, 7, 126, 145, 151, 129

3, 4, 6, 14

11, 29, 44, 145, 146, 147, 151, 2, 10

11, 29, 44, 145, 146, 147, 2, 10

Harold Washington Library Center

146, 2, 10

6, 146, 2, 10

145, 147, 151

Congress Plaza

Congress Plaza

146, 2, 10

1, 7, 126, 129

1, 7, 126

Buckingham Fountain

6, 146, 2, 10

6, 146, 2, 10

E Balbo Ave.

1, 3, 4, 129

1, 3, 4, 129

E 8th St.

S Holden Ct.

29, 44

29, 56, 44

S State St.

29, 44

29, 44, 62

29, 44, 62

S Wabash Ave.

E 9th St.

S Michigan Ave.

E 11th St.

E Balbo Dr.

6, 146, 2, 10, 14

6, 146, 2, 10, 14

S Columbus Ave.

Grant Park

Lake Michigan

S Lake Shore Dr.

6, 146, 2, 10, 14

6, 146, 2, 10, 14

41

Shedd Aquarium

E Roosevelt Rd.

12

12

S Indiana Ave.

1, 3oc, 3, 129, 4, 129

1, 3oc, 3, 129

3, 3oc

29, 44, 62

29, 44, 62

Field Museum

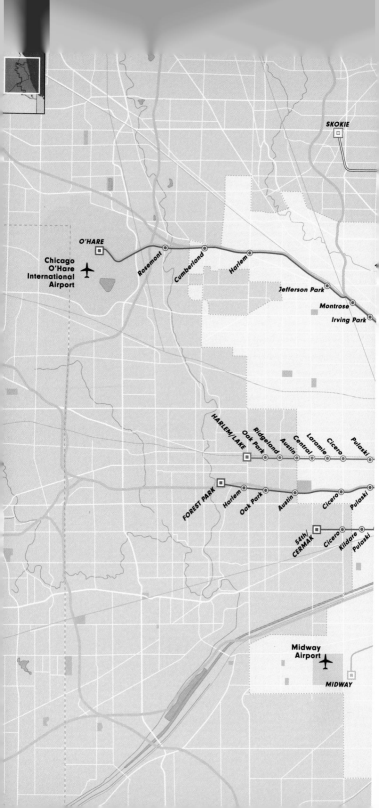

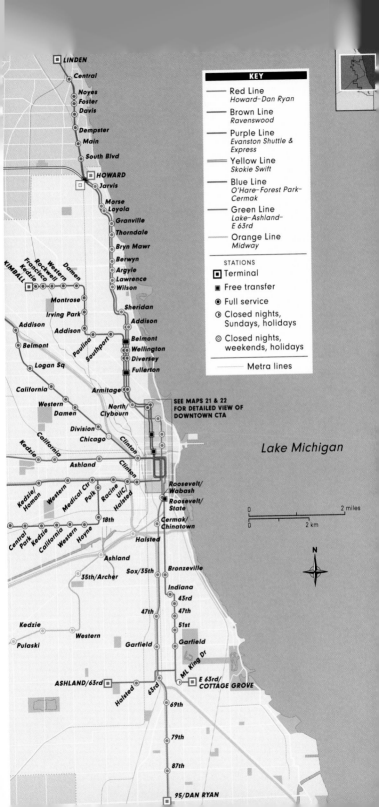

OLD TOWN

Sedgwick

KEY

CTA STATIONS
(MULT-LINE)

■ Free transfer

◩ Closed nights,
Sundays, holidays

▣ Closed nights,
weekends, holidays

CTA STATIONS
(SINGLE LINE)

◉ Full service

◑ Closed nights,
Sundays, holidays

◎ Closed nights,
weekends, holidays

▬▬▬ Metra lines

N Cleveland St.
N Hudson St.
N Sedgwick St.
N Orleans St.
N Park St.
N Wieland St.
N Wells St.
N LaSalle St.
N Parkway St.

W Schiller St.

W Sullivan St.

W Evergreen St.

W Goethe St.

W Goethe St.

W Scott St.

W Division St.

W Division St.

*Clark/
Division*

W Elm St.

*Seward
Park*

W Hill St.

W Maple St.

W Wendell St.

W Oak St.

W Walton St.

N Hudson Ave.

*Washington
Square*

W Delaware
St.

W Delaware
St.

W Locust St.

N Wells St.

W Chestnut St.

W Chestnut St.

W Institute Pl.

N State St.

■ *Chicago*

**RIVER
NORTH**

W Chicago Ave.

Chicago ◉

W Chicago Ave.

N Hudson Ave.
N Sedgwick St.
N Orleans St.
N Franklin St.

W Superior St.

N LaSalle St.
Clark St.
Dearborn St.
State St.

W Huron St.

W Erie St.

NEAR NORTH

N

W Ontario St.

W Ohio St.

0 ——— 600 feet

0 ——— 200 meters

Grand ◉

N Kingsbury St.

W Grand Ave.

CONTINUED ON MAP 22

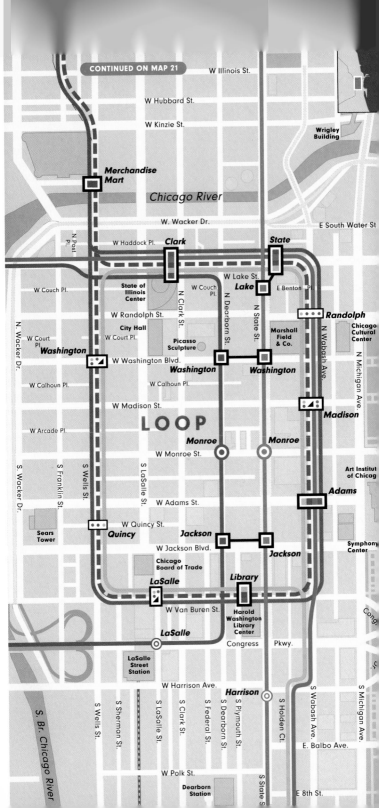

CONTINUED ON MAP 21

W Illinois St.

W Hubbard St.

W Kinzie St.

Wrigley Building

Merchandise Mart

Chicago River

W. Wacker Dr.

E South Water St

N. Post Pl.

W Haddock Pl.   **Clark**   W. Lake St.   **State**

N. Wacker Dr.

W Couch Pl.   State of Illinois Center   W Couch Pl.   **Lake**   E Benton Pl.

W Randolph St.   N Clark St.   N Dearborn St.   N State St.   **Randolph**

City Hall   W Court Pl.   Picasso Sculpture   Marshall Field & Co.   Chicago Cultural Center

W Court Pl.

Washington   W Washington Blvd.   **Washington**   **Washington**   N Wabash Ave.   N Michigan Ave.

W Calhoun Pl.   W Calhoun Pl.

W Madison St.

W Arcade Pl.   **LOOP**   **Madison**

S. Wacker Dr.   S Franklin St.   S Wells St.   S LaSalle St.   **Monroe**   **Monroe**

W Monroe St.

Art Institut of Chicag

Sears Tower   **Adams**

W Adams St.

Quincy   W Quincy St.   **Jackson**   **Jackson**   Symphony Center

Chicago Board of Trade

LaSalle   **Library**

W Van Buren St.   Harold Washington Library Center   Cong

LaSalle   Congress   Pkwy.

LaSalle Street Station

W Harrison Ave.   **Harrison**   S Holden Ct.   S Wabash Ave.   S Michigan Ave.

S. Br. Chicago River   S Wells St.   S Sherman St.   S LaSalle St.   S Clark St.   S Federal St.   S Dearborn St.   S Plymouth St.   E. Balbo Ave.

W Polk St.

Dearborn Station   S State S   E 8th St.

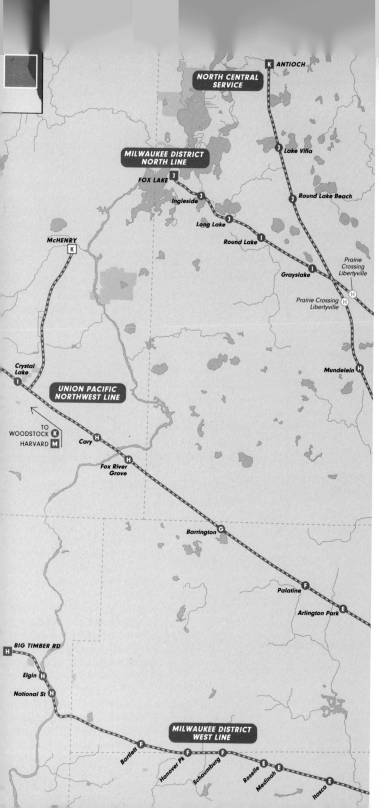

CONTINUED ON MAP 23

UNION PACIFIC
NORTHWEST LINE

Des Plaines **D**

NORTH CENTRAL
SERVICE

TO
BIG TIMBER RD **H**
ELGIN **H**
NATIONAL ST **H**

MILWAUKEE DISTRICT
WEST LINE

O'Hare Transfer **D**

Bartlett **F**

Hanover Pk **F**

Schaumburg **F**

Roselle **E**

Medinah **E**

Itasca **E**

Wood Dale **E**

Bensenville **D**

Chicago
O'Hare
International
Airport

Mannheim **C**

Franklin Park **C**

TO GENEVA **H**

UNION PACIFIC
WEST LINE

W Chicago **F**

Winfield **F**

Wheaton **E**

College Av **E**

Glen Ellyn **E**

Lombard **D**

Villa Park **D**

Elmhurst **C**

Berkeley **C**

Bellwood **C**

Melrose Park **C**

LaGrange Rd **D**

Stone Av

Western Springs

Highlands

W Hinsdale

Hinsdale **D**

Clarendon Hills **D**

Westmont **E**

Fairview Av **E**

Downers Grove
Main **E**

Belmont **E**

Lisle **E**

Napervile **F**

Rte 59 **G**

TO AURORA **H**

BURLINGTON NORTHERN
SANTA FE

Willow
Springs **D**

KEY

━━━ Metra commuter lines

STATIONS
A Terminal
A Full service
B Partial service
H Under construction
(letters indicate
fare zone)
━━━ CTA lines

Lemont **E**

153rd St/
Orland Park **E**

Lockport **G**

HERITAGE CORRIDOR

SOUTHWEST SERVICE

179th ST/
ORLAND PARK **F**

ROCK ISLAND DISTRICT

Mokena **F**

JOLIET UNION STATION **H**

New Lenox **G**

**Listed by
Site Number**

1 Wrigley Field
2 Lincoln Park
3 Nature Museum
4 Lincoln Park Zoo
5 Second City
6 Chicago Historical
  Society
7 Oak Street Beach
8 Magnificent Mile
9 John Hancock
  Observatory
10 Water Tower Place
11 Chicago Water
  Tower and Pumping
  Station
12 Museum of
  Contemporary Art
13 River North Gallery
  District
14 Navy Pier
15 Tribune Tower
16 Michigan Avenue
  Bridge
17 State of Illinois
  Center
18 *Untitled,* Picasso
19 Marshall Field & Co
20 Chicago Cultural
  Center
21 Art Institute
22 Symphony Center
23 The Rookery
24 Chicago Board of
  Trade
25 Sears Tower
26 Harold Washington
  Library Center
27 Grant Park
28 Skyline View
29 Field Museum of
  Natural Museum
30 John G Shedd
  Aquarium
31 Checkerboard
  Lounge
32 DuSable Museum of
  African American
  History
33 University of
  Chicago
34 Robie House
35 Museum of Science
  and Industry

Listed Alphabetically

Art Institute of Chicago, 21.
S Michigan Ave & E Adams St
☎ 443-3600

Checkerboard Lounge, 31.
423 E 43rd St ☎ 773/624-3240

Chicago Board of Trade, 24.
141 W Jackson ☎ 433-3590

Chicago Cultural Center, 20.
78 E Washington St ☎ 913-9446

Chicago Historical Society, 6.
1601 N Clark St ☎ 773/642-4600

Chicago Water Tower and Pumping Station, 11. 806 & 811 N Michigan Ave

DuSable Museum of African American History, 32.
☎ 773/947-0600
740 E 56th Pl

Field Museum of Natural History, 29. Roosevelt Rd and Lake Shore Dr
☎ 922-9410

Grant Park, 27. Lakefront, Roosevelt Rd to Randolph Rd

Harold Washington Library Center, 26. 400 S State St ☎ 747-4300

John G Shedd Aquarium, 30. 1200 S Lake Shore Dr ☎ 939-2438

John Hancock Observatory, 9.
875 N Michigan Ave ☎ 751-3681

Lincoln Park, 2.
Hollywood Ave to North Ave

Lincoln Park Zoo, 4.
2200 N Cannon Dr ☎ 742-2000

Magnificent Mile, 8.
Michigan Ave, Kinzie St to Oak St

Marshall Field & Co, 19.
111 N State St ☎ 781-1000

Michigan Avenue Bridge, 16.
Chicago River at E Wacker Dr

Museum of Contemporary Art, 12.
220 E Chicago Ave ☎ 280-2660

Museum of Science and Industry, 35. 57th St and Lake Shore Dr
☎ 773/684-1414

Nature Museum, Chicago Academy of Science, 3. Fullerton Pkwy & Cannon Dr ☎ 773/871-2668

Navy Pier, 14. 600 E Grand Ave
☎ 595-PIER

Oak Street Beach, 7.
600N-1600N, Lakefront

River North Gallery District, 13.
Orleans to Wells Sts, Erie St to Chicago Ave

Robie House, 34.
5757 S Woodlawn Ave
☎ 708/848-1976

The Rookery, 23.
209 S LaSalle St

Sears Tower, 25.
233 S Wacker Dr ☎ 875-9696

Second City, 5.
1616 N Wells St ☎ 337-3992

Skyline View, 28.
Lake Shore Dr and 12th St

State of Illinois Center, 17.
100 W Randolph St

Symphony Center, 22.
220 S Michigan Ave ☎ 294-3000

Tribune Tower, 15.
435 N Michigan Ave

University of Chicago, 33.
5801 S Ellis Ave
☎ 773/702-1234

***Untitled,* Picasso, 18.**
W Washington St at N Dearborn

Water Tower Place, 10.
835 N Michigan Ave ☎ 440-3166.

Wrigley Field, 1. 1060 W Addison St
☎ 773/404-2827

Listed by Site Number

31 Uptown Theatre

32 Uptown Bank Bldg

33 Hutchinson Street Landmark District

34 H Rokham House

35 Elks National Monument Building

36 St Clement's Church

37 Reebie Storage & Moving Co

38 Crilly Court

39 1500 N Astor St

40 Albert Madlener Residence

41 151 W Burton Place

42 Holy Trinity Cathedral

43 St. John Cantius

44 Charnley-Persky House

45 Carl C. Heisen House

46 Newberry Library

47 Archbishop Quigley Prep School

48 John Hancock Building

49 860–880 N Lake Shore Dr

50 Chicago Water Tower/Pumping Stn

51 St. James Episcopal Cathedral

52 Medinah Temple

53 Tribune Tower

54 Wrigley Building

55 Michigan Avenue Br

56 Centennial Fountain and Arc

57 University of Illinois Chicago Campus

58 Second Presbyterian Church

59 J J Glessner House

60 W W Kimball Hse

61 Monument to the Great Migration

62 Illinois Institute of Technology Campus

63 I Heller House

64 Univ of Chicago Quadrangles

65 Robie House

66 South Shore Cultural Center

67 Pullman

Listed by Site Number

1 Marina City	**12** Chicago Temple	**21** Harold Washington Library Center
2 75 E Wacker Dr	**13** Civic Opera Building	
3 Carbon and Carbide Building	**14** Old St. Patrick's	**22** Monadnock Building
4 35 E Wacker Dr	**15** *Dawn Shadows*	**23** *Flamingo*
5 333 W Wacker Dr	**16** Sears Tower	**24** Marquette Building
6 State of Illinois Ctr	**17** 134 S LaSalle St	**25** *The Four Seasons*
7 Chicago Theater	**18** The Rookery	**26** Inland Steel Building
8 Chicago Cultural Ctr	**19** Chicago Board of Trade	**27** Carson Pirie Scott & Co
9 Reliance Building	**20** Chicago Metropolitan Correction Center	**28** Santa Fe Center
10 *Miss Chicago*		**29** Auditorium Building
11 *Untitled*		**30** Buckingham Fountain

Listed Alphabetically

Albert Madlener Residence, (Graham Foundation for Advanced Studies in the Fine Arts), 40.
4 W Burton Pl ☎ 573-1365

Archbishop Quigley Preparatory Seminary, 47. Pearson and Rush Sts ☎ 787-9343

Auditorium Building, 29.
430 S Michigan Ave

Buckingham Fountain, 30.
Congress Dr at Columbus Dr

Carbon and Carbide Building, 3.
230 N Michigan Ave

Carl C Heisen House, 45.
1250 N Lake Shore Dr

Carson Pirie Scott & Co, 27.
1 S State St ☎ 641-7000

Centennial Fountain and Arc, 56.
300 E McClurg Court

Charnley-Persky House, 44.
1365 N Astor St ☎ 573-1365

Chicago Board of Trade Building, 19. 141 W Jackson Blvd ☎ 435-3590

Chicago Cultural Center, 8.
78 E Washington St ☎ 913-9446

Chicago Metropolitan Correctional Center, 20. 71 W Van Buren St

Chicago Temple (First United Methodist Church of Chicago), 12.
77 W Washington St ☎ 236-4548

Chicago Theater, 7. 175 N State St

Chicago Water Tower and Pumping Station, 50. 806 & 811 N Michigan Ave

Civic Opera Building, 13.
20 N Wacker Dr

Crilly Court, 38. North Park Ave & Wells St, St Paul Ave & Eugenie

Listed Alphabetically

***Dawn Shadows,* Nevelson, 15.**
200 W Madison St

860-880 N Lake Shore Dr, 49.

**Elks National Memorial
Building, 35.** 2750 N Lakeview Ave
☎ 773/477-2750

**1500 N Astor St (Patterson-
McCormick Mansion), 39.**
20 E Burton Place

***Flamingo,* Calder, 23.** Dearborn St
between Adams & Jackson Sts

***The Four Seasons,* Chagall, 25.**
Dearborn and Monroe Sts

Frederick C Robie House, 65.
5757 S Woodlawn Ave
☎ 708/848-1976

**Harold Washington Library
Center, 21.** 400 S State St
☎ 747-4300

Henry Rohkam House, 34.
1048 W Oakdale Ave

Holy Trinity Cathedral, 42.
1121 N Leavitt St ☎ 773/486-4545

**Hutchinson Street Landmark
District, 33.** Hutchinson St between
Marine Dr & Hazel St

**Illinois Institute of Technology
Campus, 62.** S Michigan Ave to IC
Tracks, 31st to 35th Sts

Inland Steel Building, 26.
30 W Monroe St

Isidore Heller House, 63.
5132 S Woodlawn Ave

John Hancock Building, 48.
875 N Michigan Ave ☎ 888/875-VIEW

John J Glessner House, 59.
1800 S Prairie Ave

Marina City, 1. 300 N State St

Marquette Building, 24.
140 S Dearborn St

Medinah Temple, 52.
600 N Wabash Ave

Michigan Avenue Bridge, 55.
Chicago River at E. Wacker Dr

***Miss Chicago,* Miro, 10.**
Washington and Dearborn Sts

Monadnock Building, 22.
53 W Jackson Blvd

**Monument to the Great
Migration, 61.** 26th Pl and Martin
Luther King Dr

Newberry Library, 46.
60 W Walton St ☎ 943-9090

**Old St Patrick's Roman Catholic
Church, 14.** 700 W Adams St
☎ 648-1021

151 W Burton Place, 41. Burton Place
between LaSalle & Wells Sts

135 S LaSalle St, 17. LaSalle &
Adams Sts

Pullman, 67. 111th and 115th Sts,
Cottage Grove and Langley Aves
☎ 773/785-8181

Reebie Storage & Moving Co., 37.
2325 N Clark St

Reliance Building, 9. 32 N State St

The Rookery, 18. 209 S LaSalle St

St Clement's Church, 36. 646 W
Deming Place ☎ 773/281-0431

St James Episcopal Cathedral, 51.
65 E Huron ☎ 787-7360.

**St John Cantius Roman Catholic
Church, 43.** 825 N Carpenter St
☎ 243-7373

Santa Fe Center, 28.
80 E Jackson Blvd

Sears Tower, 16.
233 S Wacker Dr ☎ 875-9696

Second Presbyterian Church, 58.
1936 S Michigan Ave ☎ 225-4951

75 E Wacker Dr, 2.

South Shore Cultural Center, 66.
7059 S Shore Dr ☎ 773/747-2536

State of Illinois Center, 6.
100 W Randolph St

35 E Wacker Dr, 4.

333 W Wacker Dr, 5.

Tribune Tower, 53.
435 N Michigan Ave

**University of Chicago
Quadrangles, 64.** Ellis and University
Aves, E 57th and E 59th Sts

**University of Illinois at Chicago
Campus, 57.** Eisenhower Expwy to
Roosevelt Rd, Halsted to Racine Sts

***Untitled,* Picasso, 11.**
Washington and Dearborn Sts

Uptown Broadway Building, 32.
4707 N Broadway

Uptown Theatre, 31.
4814 N Broadway

William W Kimball House, 60.
1801 S Prairie Ave

Wrigley Building, 54.
400-410 N Michigan Ave

Listed by Site Number

1 O B Balch Home
2 W C Fricke Home
3 Edwin C Cheney Home
4 Rollin Furbeck Home
5 Frank Lloyd Wright Home and Studio
6 R P Parker Home
7 T H Gale Home
8 Walter H Gale Home
9 Moore-Dugal Home
10 A B Heurtley Home
11 Mrs. T. H. Gale Home
12 Ernest Hemingway Birthplace
13 Edward W McCready Home
14 G W Furbeck Home
15 Hemingway Museum
16 F W Thomas Home
17 Oak Park Visitor's Center
18 Unity Temple
19 Historical Society of Oak Park & River Forest
20 Pleasant Home
21 Oak Park Conservatory
22 Brookfield Zoo

Listed Alphabetically

Arthur B Heurtley Home, 10. 318 N Forest Ave

Brookfield Zoo, 22. First Ave & 31st St, Brookfield ☎ 708/485-0263

Edward W McCready Home, 13. 231 N Euclid Ave

Edwin H Cheney Home, 3. 520 N East Ave

Ernest Hemingway Birthplace, 12. 339 N Oak Park Ave ☎ 708/848-2222

Ernest Hemingway Museum, 15. 200 N Oak Park Ave ☎ 708/848-2222

Frank Lloyd Wright Home and Studio, 5. 951 Chicago Ave ☎ 708/848-1976

Frank W Thomas Home, 16. 210 N Forest Ave

George W Furbeck Home, 14. 223 N Euclid Ave

Historical Society of Oak Park & River Forest, 19. 217 S Home Ave ☎ 708/848-6755

Moore-Dugal Home, 9. 333 N Forest Ave

Mrs Thomas H Gale Home, 11. 6 Elizabeth Court

Oak Park Conservatory, 21. 615 W Garfield St ☎ 708/386-4700

Oak Park Visitor's Center, 17. 158 N Forest Ave ☎ 708/848-1500

Oscar B Balch Home, 1. 611 N Kenilworth Ave

Pleasant Home (John Farson Home), 20. 217 S Home Ave ☎ 708/383-2654

Robert P Parker Home, 6. 1019 W Chicago Ave

Rollin Furbeck Home, 4. 515 N Fair Oaks Ave

Thomas H Gale Home, 7. 1027 W Chicago Ave

Unity Temple, 18. 875 Lake St ☎ 708/383-8873

Walter H Gale Home, 8. 1031 W Chicago Ave

William C Fricke Home, 2. 540 N Fair Oaks Ave

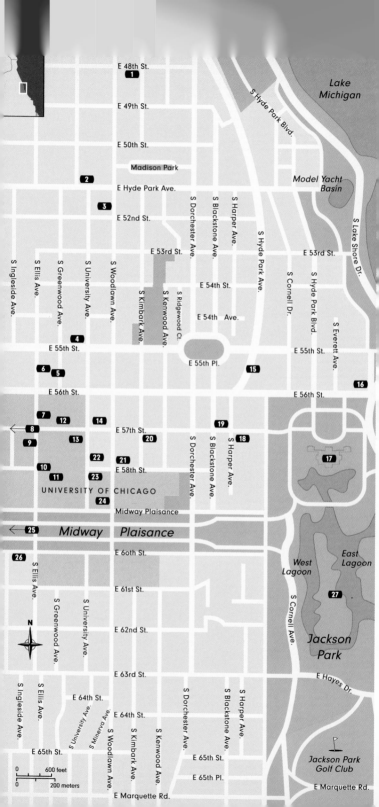

Listed by Site Number

1 George L Miller House
2 KAM Isaiah Israel Congregation
3 Isidore Heller House
4 Lutheran School of Theology
5 David and Alfred Smart Museum of Art
6 Court Theatre
7 *Nuclear Energy*, Moore
8 DuSable Museum of African American History
9 John Crerar Library
10 Cobb Hall
10 Renaissance Society
11 Bond Chapel
12 Joseph Regenstein Library
13 Mandel Hall
14 First Unitarian Church of Chicago
15 Hyde Park Historical Society
16 Promontory Apartments
17 Museum of Science and Industry
18 Powell's Bookstore
19 O'Gara & Wilson Booksellers
20 57th Street Books
21 Frederick C Robie House
22 Seminary Co-Op Bookstore
22 Chicago Theological Seminary
23 Oriental Institute
24 Rockefeller Memorial Chapel
25 *Fountain of Time*, Taft
26 School of Social Service Administration
27 Jackson Park

Listed Alphabetically

Bond Chapel, 11. 1025 E 58th St

Chicago Theological Seminary, 22. 5757 S University Ave ☎ 773/752-5757

Cobb Hall, 10. 5811 S Ellis Ave

Court Theatre, 6. 5535 S Ellis Ave ☎ 773/753-4472

David and Alfred Smart Museum of Art, 5. 5500 S Greenwood Ave ☎ 773/702-0200

DuSable Museum of African American History, 8. 740 E 56th Pl ☎ 773/947-0600

57th Street Books, 20. 1301 E 57th St ☎ 773/684-1300

First Unitarian Church of Chicago, 14. 5650 S Woodlawn Ave ☎ 773/324-4100

Fountain of Time, Taft, 25. Midway Plaisance, West of Cottage Grove Ave

Frederick C Robie House, 21. 5757 S Woodlawn Ave ☎ 708/848-1976

George L Miller House, 1. 4800 S Kimbark Ave

Hyde Park Historical Society, 15. 5529 S Lake Park Ave ☎ 773/493-1893

Isidore Heller House, 3. 5132 S Woodlawn Ave

Jackson Park, 27. E 56th-67th Sts, S Stony Island to Lake Michigan

John Crerar Library, 9. 5730 S Ellis Ave ☎ 773/702-7715

Joseph Regenstein Library, 12. 1100 E 57th St

KAM Isaiah Israel Congregation, 2. 1100 E Hyde Park Blvd ☎ 773/924-1234

Lutheran School of Theology, 4. 1100 E 55th St ☎ 773/753-0700

Mandel Hall, 13. 1131 E 57th St ☎ 773/702-7300

Museum of Science and Industry, 17. 5700 S Lake Shore Dr ☎ 773/684-1414

Nuclear Energy, Moore, 7. Ellis Ave between 56th & 57th Sts

O'Gara & Wilson Booksellers, 19. 1448 E 57th St ☎ 773/363-0993

Oriental Institute, 23. 1155 E 58th St ☎ 773/702-9520

Powell's Bookstore, 18. 1501 E 57th St ☎ 773/955-7780

Promontory Apartments, 16. 5530 S South Shore Dr

Renaissance Society, 10. 5811 S Ellis Ave ☎ 773/702-8670

Rockefeller Memorial Chapel, 24. 5850 S Woodlawn Ave ☎ 773/702-2100.

School of Social Service Administration, 26. 969 E 60th St

Seminary Co-Op Bookstore, 22. 5757 S University Ave ☎ 773/752-4381

Listed by Site Number

1 Chicago Botanic Garden

2 Kohl Children's Museum

3 Baha'i House of Worship

4 Kendall-Mitchell Museum of the American Indian

5 Ladd Memorial Arboretum and Ecology Center

6 Grosse Pointe Lighthouse and Maritime Museum

7 Shakespeare Garden

8 Mary and Leigh Block Gallery

9 Northwestern University

10 Northwestern University Visitor Center

11 Frances E Willard House/National Women's Christian Temperance Union Headquarters

12 Merrick Rose Garden

13 Evanston Historical Society/Charles G Dawes Home

Listed Alphabetically

Baha'i House of Worship, 3. 100 Linden Ave, Wilmette ☎ 847/853-2300

Chicago Botanic Garden, 1. Lake Cook Road and Rte. 41, Glencoe ☎ 847/835-5440

Evanston Historical Society/Charles G Dawes Home, 13. 225 Greenwood Ave ☎ 847/475-3410

Frances E Willard House/National Women's Christian Temperance Union Headquarters, 11. 1730 Chicago Ave ☎ 847/864-1396

Grosse Pointe Lighthouse and Maritime Museum, 6. 2601 N. Sheridan Rd ☎ 847/328-6961

Kendall-Mitchell Museum of the American Indian, 4. 2600 Central Park ☎ 847/475-1030

Kohl Children's Museum, 2. 165 Green Bay Road, Wilmette ☎ 847/256-6056

Ladd Memorial Arboretum and Ecology Center, 5. 2024 McCormick Rd ☎ 847/864-5181

Mary and Leigh Block Gallery, 8. 1967 South Campus Drive ☎ 847/491-4000

Merrick Rose Garden, 12. Oak Ave & Lake St ☎ 847/866-2911

Northwestern University, 9. 1801 Hinman Ave ☎ 847/491-3741

Northwestern University Visitor Center, 10. 1800 Sheridan Rd ☎ 847/491-7200

7200 Shakespeare Garden, 7. 2121 Sheridan Rd

Church St.

Davis St.

Arcadia St.

Grove St.

Devonshire Cultural Center

Lake St.

Greenwood Ave.

Turner Ln.

Dempster St.

58

Crain St.

Evanston Golf Club

Greenleaf Ave.

Elm Terr.

Lee St.

Bobolink Terr.

Main

1

Madison St.

James Dr.

Cleveland St.

Keeney St.

Oakton St.

Kirk St.

4

Oakton Park

3

Mulford St.

Mulford St.

Brummel St.

Hamlin Park

Howard St.

Birchwood Ave.

Jarvis Ave.

Chase Ave.

Lincoln Ave.

Touhy Ave.

41

Estes Ave.

Lunt Ave.

Fitch Ave.

Fairview Ln.

Coyle Ave.
Morse Ave.
Farwell Ave.

94

Pratt Ave.

Gross Point Rd.

Laramine Ave.

LeClaire Ave.

Niles Center Rd.

Skokie Blvd.

41

Kenton Ave.
Knox Ave.
Kilpatrick Ave.
Keating Ave.

Kildare Ave.
Kostner Ave.
Kenneth Ave.
Kilbourn Ave.
Kolmar Ave.

Tripp Ave.
Lowell Ave.

Crawford Ave.

Kedvale Ave.
Karlov Ave.
Keeler Ave.

Keystone Ave.
Harding Ave.

Springfield Ave.

East Prairie Rd.

Central Park Ave.
Monticello Ave.
Lawndale Ave.
Ridgway Ave.
Hamlin Ave.

Kimball Ave.
Trumball Ave.
St. Louis Ave.
Drake Ave.

Mc Daniel Ave.

McCormick Blvd.

Christiana Ave.

2

5

LaVergne Ave.

LeClaire Ave.

Fargo Ave.

50

McCormick Blvd.

N

| 0 | | 1800 feet |
| 0 | | 600 meters |

Listed by Site Number

1 Holocaust Memorial Museum
2 Skokie Northshore Sculpture Park
3 Emily Oaks Nature Center
4 The Exploritorium
5 Skokie Heritage Museum and Log Cabin/Skokie Historical Society

---

Listed Alphabetically

Emily Oaks Nature Center, 3.
4650 Brummel St
☎ 847/674-1500, ext 8

The Exploritorium, 4.
4701 Oakton St ☎ 847/674-1500, ext 5

Holocaust Memorial Foundation Museum, 1. 4255 Main St
☎ 847/677-4640

Skokie Heritage Museum and Log Cabin, 5. 8031 Floral Ave
☎ 847/677-6672

Skokie Historical Society, 5. 8031 Floral Ave ☎ 847/673-1888

Skokie Northshore Sculpture Park, 2. McCormick Blvd between Dempster St and Touhy Ave
☎ 847/583-8549

Listed by Site Number

1 Willie Dixon's Blues Heaven

2 Quinn Chapel AME Church

3 Chicago Defender

4 Monument to the Great Migration

5 *Victory*

6 Chicago Bee

7 Chicago Urban League/Swift Mansion

8 Oscar Stanton De Priest Home

9 Elijah Muhammad Home

10 Operation PUSH

11 DuSable Museum of African American History

12 Oak Woods Cemetery

13 Mosque Maryam

14 A Philip Randolph Pullman Porter National Museum

Listed Alphabetically

A Philip Randolph Pullman Porter National Museum, 14.
10406 S Maryland Ave
☎ 773/928-3935

Chicago Bee Building, 6.
3647-55 S State St

Chicago Defender Building, 3.
2400 S Michigan Ave ☎ 225-2400

Chicago Urban League/Swift Mansion, 7. 4500 S Michigan Ave

DuSable Museum of African American History, 11.
740 E 56th Pl ☎ 773/947-0600

Elijah Muhammad Home, 9.
S Woodlawn Ave and 49th St

Monument to the Great Migration, 4. 26th Pl and Martin Luther King Dr

Mosque Maryam, 13. 7351 S Stony Island Ave ☎ 773/324-6000

Oak Woods Cemetery, 12. 67th St and Cottage Grove Ave
☎ 773/288-3800

Operation PUSH, 10. 930 E 50th St
☎ 773/373-3366

Oscar Stanton De Priest Home, 8.
4536-38 S Martin L King Dr

Quinn Chapel A.M.E Church, 2.
2401 S. Wabash Ave ☎ 791-1846

Victory, Monument for the 93rd Division, 5. Martin Luther King Dr at 35th St

Willie Dixon's Blues Heaven, 1.
2120 S Michigan Ave ☎ 808-1286

Listed by Site Number

1 Ner Tamid Congregation of North Town

2 Edgewater Presbyterian Church

3 St Ita's Church

4 All Saints Episcopal Church

5 Islamic Center of Chicago

6 St Mary of the Lake

7 Graceland Cemetery

8 Temple Sholom

9 Our Lady of Mount Carmel Church

10 St Alphonsus Redemptorist

11 Wellington Ave United Church of Christ

12 St Clement's Church

13 St Paul's United Church of Christ

14 Church of Our Savior

15 St Vincent de Paul Church

16 St Mary of the Angels

17 First Bethlehem Lutheran Church

18 Midwest Buddhist Temple

19 St Michael's Church

20 Moody Memorial Church

21 St Chrysostom's Episcopal Church

22 Holy Trinity Cathedral

23 St Nicholas Ukranian Catholic Cathedral

24 Lake Shore Drive Synagogue

25 Chicago Sinai Congregation

26 Fourth Presbyterian Church

27 Holy Name Cathedral

28 St James Cathedral

29 Seventeenth Church of Christ Scientist

30 First United Methodist Church

31 St Peter's Church

32 Chicago Loop Synagogue

33 Old St. Patrick's Church

34 First Baptist Congregational

35 St Stephen's AME Church

36 Greek Orthodox Church of St Basil

37 Second Presbyterian Church

38 Quinn Chapel AME

39 Olivet Baptist Church

40 Grant Memorial AME Church

41 KAM Isaiah Israel Congregation

42 First Unitarian Church of Chicago

43 Rockefeller Memorial Chapel

44 Oak Woods Cemetery

45 Mosque Maryam

Listed Alphabetically

All Saints Episcopal Church, 4.
4550 N Hermitage Ave
☎ 773/561-0111

Chicago Loop Synagogue, 32.
16 S Clark St ☎ 346-7370. Traditional Jewish

Chicago Sinai Congregation, 25.
15 W Delaware Pl ☎ 867-7000. Reform Jewish

Church of Our Savior, 14. 530 W Fullerton Pkwy ☎ 773/549-3832. Episcopal

Edgewater Presbyterian Church, 2.
1020 W Bryn Mawr Ave
☎ 773/561-4748

First Baptist Congregational Church, 34. 1613 W Washington St
☎ 243-8047

First Bethlehem Lutheran Church, 17.
1649 W LeMoyne St ☎ 773/276-2338

First Unitarian Church of Chicago, 42. 5650 S Woodlawn Ave
☎ 773/324-4100

First United Methodist Church of Chicago, 30. 77 W Washington St
☎ 236-4548

Fourth Presbyterian Church, 26.
866 N Michigan Ave ☎ 787-4570

Grant Memorial AME Church, 40.
4017 S Drexel Blvd ☎ 773/285-5819

Greek Orthodox Church of St. Basil, 36. 733 S Ashland Ave
☎ 243-3738

Listed Alphabetically

Holy Name Cathedral, 27.
735 N State St ☎ 787–8040. Roman Catholic

Holy Trinity Cathedral, 22.
1121 N. Leavitt St ☎ 773/486–4545. Russian Orthodox

Islamic Center of Chicago, 5.
4033 N Damen ☎ 773/477–0003

KAM Isaiah Israel Congregation, 41. 1100 E Hyde Park Blvd
☎ 773/924–1234. Reform Jewish

Lake Shore Drive Synagogue, 24.
70 E Elm St ☎ 337–6811. Traditional Jewish

Midwest Buddist Temple, 18.
435 Menomonee St ☎ 943–7801

Moody Memorial Church, 20.
1609 N LaSalle Dr ☎ 943–0466. Non-denominational

Mosque Maryam, 45.
7351 S Stony Island Ave
☎ 773/324–6000. Nation of Islam

Ner Tamid Congregation of North Town, 1. 2754 W Rosemont Ave
☎ 773/465–6090. Conservative Jewish

Old St. Patrick's Church, 33.
700 W Adams St ☎ 648–1021. Roman Catholic

Olivet Baptist Church, 39.
3101 S Martin Luther King Dr
☎ 842–1081

Our Lady of Mount Carmel Church, 9. 690 W Belmont Ave
☎ 773/525–0453. Roman Catholic

Quinn Chapel AME, 38.
2401 S Wabash ☎ 791–1846

Rockefeller Memorial Chapel, 43.
5850 S Woodlawn Ave
☎ 773/702–2100. Ecumenical

St Alphonsus Redemptrist Church, 10. 1429 W Welllington Ave
☎ 773/525–0709. Roman Catholic

St Chrysostom's Episcopal Church, 21. 1424 N Dearborn St
☎ 944–1083

St Clement's Church, 12. 642 W. Deming Pl ☎ 773/281–0431. Roman Catholic

St Ita's Church, 3.
1220 W Catalpa Ave ☎ 773/561–5343. Roman Catholic

St James Cathedral, 28.
65 E Huron St ☎ 787–7360. Episcopal

St Mary of the Angels Church, 16. 1850 N Hermitage Ave
☎ 773/278–2644. Roman Catholic

St Mary of the Lake, 6.
4200 N Sheridan Rd ☎ 773/472–3711. Roman Catholic

St Michael's Church, 19.
447 W Eugenie St ☎ 642–2498. Roman Catholic

St Nicholas Ukranian Catholic Cathedral, 23. 2238 W Rice St
☎ 773/276–4537

St Paul's United Church of Christ, 13. 2335 N Orchard St
☎ 773/348–3829

St Peter's Church, 31.
110 W Madison St ☎ 372–5111. Roman Catholic

St Stephen's AME Church, 35.
2000 W Washington Blvd ☎ 666–4164

St Vincent de Paul Church, 15.
1010 W Webster Ave ☎ 773/327–1113. Roman Catholic

Second Presbyterian Church, 37.
1936 S Michigan Ave ☎ 225–4951

Seventeenth Church of Christ Scientist, 29. 55 E Wacker Dr
☎ 236–4671

Temple Sholom, 8.
3480 N Lake Shore Dr
☎ 773/525–4707. Reform Jewish

Wellington Ave United Church of Christ, 11. 615 W Wellington Ave
☎ 773/935–0642

CEMETERIES

Graceland Cemetery, 7.
4001 N Clark St ☎ 773/525–1105

Oak Woods Cemetery, 44.
1035 E 67th St ☎ 773/288–3800

Diversey Harbor

3

Lincoln Ave.

Clark St.

Fullerton Ave.

N. 2400N

N. Branch Chicago R.

DePaul U

DEPAUL

Armitage Ave.

Clybourn Ave.

Milwaukee Ave.

Lincoln Park Zoo

2000N

LINCOLN PARK

4

North Ave.

North Ave. 1600N

5

LaSalle St.

State St.

WICKER PARK

North Ave.

Division St.

WEST TOWN

Halsted St.

Stanton Park

Division St. 1200N

Western Ave.

2400W

2000W

1600W

1200W

Chicago Ave.

800N

7

Leavitt St.

Damen Ave.

Wood St.

Ashland Ave.

Ogden Ave.

6

NEAR NORTH

8

Water Tower

9

11

10

800N

400W

Michigan Ave.

NEAR NORTH

12

Navy Pier

400N

Kinzie St.

Lake St.

400N

Wacker Dr.

1W 1E

14

15

Lake Shore Dr.

Union Park

13

NEAR WEST SIDE

United Center

001N

001S

Madison St.

Adams St.

16

Grant Park

Eisenhower Expwy.

Jackson Blvd.

290

1N

1S

Wacker Dr.

Dan Ryan Expwy.

LOOP

State St.

17

18

400S

800S

Ogden Ave.

UNIVERSITY VILLAGE

University of Illinois/Chicago

19

Racine Ave.

Halsted St.

Roosevelt Rd.

Roosevelt Rd.

1200S

Canal St.

20

Shedd Aquarium

22

Field Museum

21

Soldier Field

1W 1E

NEAR SOUTH SIDE

2000S

Harrison Park

24

1600S

1200S

800W

23

Cermak Rd.

CHINA-TOWN

2200S

2400S

McCormick Place

Western Ave.

2400W

Damen Ave.

Ashland Ave.

S. Branch Chicago R.

55

Archer Ave.

PILSEN

McGurne Park

BRIDGEPORT

31st St.

2800S

90

94

400W

200E

400E

41

DOUGLAS

3100S

Sherman Park

McKINLEY PARK

35th St.

Halsted St.

Wallace Ave.

Armour Park

Illinois Institute of Technology

Indiana Ave.

3500S

Ellis Park

OAKLAND

Western Ave.

Comiskey Park

Dan Ryan Expwy.

3900S

State St.

Michigan Ave.

Pershing Rd.

Martin Luther King Jr. Dr.

43rd St.

Drexel Ave.

Washington Park

26

S Ellis Ave.

25

S Woodlawn Ave.

S Dorchester Ave.

E 55th St.

4300S

S Martin Luther King Jr. Dr.

S Cottage Grove Ave.

28

29

University of Chicago

Midway Plaisance Park

E 60th St.

27

Jackson Park

Hyde Park Area

4700S

TO HYDE PARK

N

1 mile

1 km

Meigs Field

Listed by Site Number

3   Nature Museum
4   Chicago Historical Society
5   International Museum of Surgical Science
6   Polish Museum of America
7   Ukranian National Museum
8   Peace Museum
9   Museum of Contemporary Art
10 ABA Museum of Law
11 Terra Museum of American Art
12 Chicago Children's Museum
13 Museum of Holography
14 Museum of Broadcast Communications
15 Chicago Athenaeum Museum of Architecture and Design
16 Art Institute of Chicago
17 Museum of Contemporary Photography
18 Spertus Museum of Judaica
19 Hull House Museum
20 John G. Shedd Aquarium
21 Adler Planetarium and Astronomy Museum
22 Field Museum of Natural History
23 American Police Center and Museum
24 Mexican Fine Arts Center
25 David and Alfred Smart Museum of Art
26 DuSable Museum of African American History
27 Museum of Science and Industry
28 Oriental Institute
29 Renaissance Society

Listed Alphabetically

ABA Museum of Law, 10.
750 N Lake Shore Dr ☎ 988-6222

Adler Planetarium and Astronomy Museum, 21. 1300 S Lake Shore Dr
☎ 322-0304

American Police Center and Museum, 23. 1717 S State St
☎ 431-0005

Art Institute of Chicago, 16.
S Michigan Ave & Adams St
☎ 443-3600

Chicago Athenaeum Museum of Architecture and Design, 15.
6 N Michigan Ave ☎ 251-0175

Chicago Children's Museum, 12.
Navy Pier, 700 E Grand Ave
☎ 527-1000

Chicago Historical Society, 4.
1601 N Clark St ☎ 642-4600

David and Alfred Smart Museum of Art, 25. 5500 S Greenwood Ave
☎ 773/702-0200

DuSable Museum of African American History, 26. 740 E 56th Pl
☎ 773/947-0600

Field Museum of Natural History, 22. Roosevelt Rd at Lake Shore Dr ☎ 922-9410

Hull House Museum, 19.
800 S Halsted St ☎ 413-5353

International Museum of Surgical Science, 5. 1524 Lake Shore Dr
☎ 642-6502

John G Shedd Aquarium, 20.
1200 S Lake Shore Dr ☎ 939-2438

Mexican Fine Arts Center, 24.
1852 W 19th St ☎ 738-1503

Museum of Broadcast Communications, 14.
78 E Washington St ☎ 629-6000

Museum of Contemporary Art, 9.
220 E Chicago Ave ☎ 280-2660

Museum of Contemporary Photography, 17. Columbia College,
600 S Michigan Ave ☎ 663-5554

Museum of Holography, 13.
1134 W Washington St ☎ 226-1007

Museum of Science and Industry, 27. 5700 S Lake Shore Dr
☎ 773/684-1414

Nature Museum, Chicago Academy of Science, 3. Fullerton Pkwy &
Cannon Dr ☎ 773/871-2668

Oriental Institute, 28.
1155 E 58th St ☎ 773/702-9520

Peace Museum, 8.
314 W Institute Pl ☎ 440-1860

Polish Museum of America, 6.
984 N Milwaukee Ave
☎ 773/384-3352

Renaissance Society, 29.
5811 S Ellis Ave ☎ 773/702-8670

Spertus Museum of Judaica, 18.
618 S Michigan Ave ☎ 922-9012

Terra Museum of American Art, 11.
666 N Michigan Ave ☎ 664-3939

Ukranian National Museum, 7.
721 N Oakley Blvd ☎ 421-8020

Listed by Site Number

1 Martin D'Arcy
Gallery of Art

2 Swedish-American
Museum Center

30 Balzekas Museum of
Lithuanian Culture

31 A Philip Randolph
Pullman Porter
National Museum

Listed Alphabetically

**A Philip Randolph Pullman Porter
National Museum, 31.**
10406 S Maryland Ave
☎ 773/928-3935

**Balzekas Museum of Lithuanian
Culture, 30.** 6500 S Pulaski Rd
☎ 773/582-6500

Martin D'Arcy Gallery of Art, 1.
Loyola University, 6525 N Sheridan
Ave ☎ 773/508-2679

**Swedish-American Museum
Center, 2.** 5211 N Clark St
☎ 773/728-8111

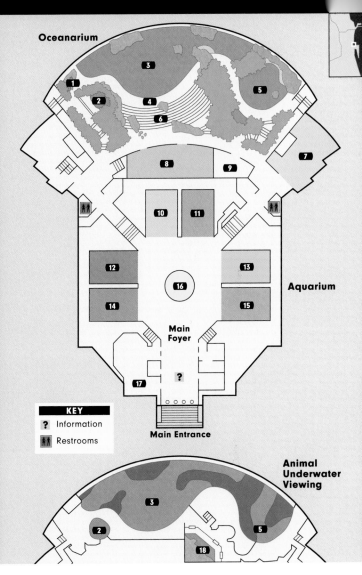

Oceanarium

Aquarium

Main Foyer

Animal Underwater Viewing

KEY	
?	Information
🚻	Restrooms

Main Entrance

Listed by Site Number

1 Tide Pool
2 Sea Otter Cove
3 Pacific White-sided Dolphins or Beluga Whales
4 Nature Trail
5 Secluded Bay/Beluga Whales or Dolphins
6 Marine Mammal Presentation Seating

7 Phelps Auditorium
8 Special Exhibit
9 Big Blue Gift Shop
10 Illinois
11 North American Coasts
12 South America
13 Indo-Pacific
14 Asia, Africa and Australia

15 The Caribbean
16 Coral Reef Dive
17 Go Overboard Gift Shop
18 Penguins

FIRST FLOOR

| 1 |
| 2 |
| 3 |
| 4 |
| 5 |
| 6 |
| 7 |
| 8 |
| 9 |
| 10 |

MEN
WOMEN

?

| 11 |
| 12 |
| 13 |
| 14 |
| 15 |
| 16 |
| 17 |
| 18 |
| 19 |
| 20 |

?

SECOND FLOOR

?

| 21 |
| 22 |
| 2 |
| 4 |

WOMEN
MEN

| 9 |
| 15 |
| 23 |

| 24 |
| 25 |
| 26 |
| 27 |
| 28 |
| 29 |
| 30 |
| 31 |
| 32 |

?

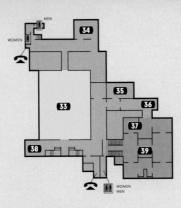

LOWER LEVEL

KEY	
?	Information
🚻	Restrooms
☎	Telephones

Listed by Site Number

1 Betty Rymer Gallery
2 The School of the Art Institute
3 Chicago Stock Exchange Trading Room
4 Arthur Rubloff Auditorium
5 McKinlock Court Garden
6 Ancient Egyptian, Greek, Etruscan, and Roman
7 American Arts 1901 to Present
8 Indian and South East Asian
9 Sculpture Court
10 American Arts to 1900
11 Arms and Armor
12 European Decorative Arts
13 African and Ancient American
14 Prints and Drawings
15 Museum Shop

16 Chinese, Japanese, and Korean
17 Contemporary
18 Print Study Room
19 Fullerton Auditorium
20 Ryerson and Burnham Libraries
21 Restaurant on the Park
22 The School of the Art Institute Film Center
23 Regenstein Hall-Special Exhibitions
24 Modern 1900-1935
25 European 1800s
26 European Prints and Drawings
27 European 1600s-1700s
28 European
29 Architecture
30 European 1400s
31 Impressionism and Post-Impressionism
32 Modern 1935-1955
33 Garden Restaurant

34 Court Cafeteria
35 Textiles Study Room
36 Textiles
37 Paperweight Collection
38 European Decorative Arts 1900s
39 European Decorative Arts 1600-1900
40 Architecture Study Room
41 Architecture
42 Morton Auditorium
43 Photography
44 Photography Study Room
45 Thorne Miniature Rooms
46 Kraft Education Center
47 Price Auditorium

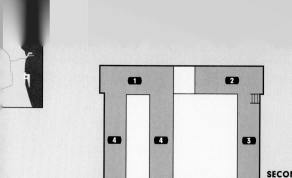

SECOND FLOOR

KEY

? Information

Restrooms

Telephones

MEN

WOMEN

MEN

WOMEN

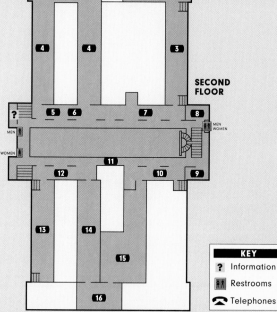

FIRST FLOOR

WOMEN

WOMEN

MEN

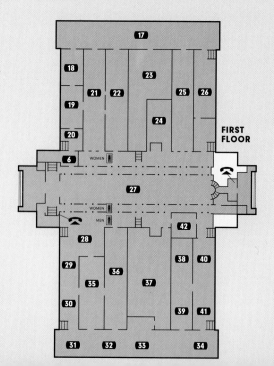

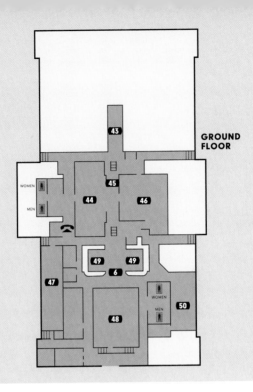

GROUND FLOOR

Listed by Site Number

1 Elizabeth Morse Genius Dinosaur Hall
2 Plants
3 Plants of the World
4 Life Over Time
5 Moving Earth
6 Museum Store
7 Families at Work
8 Jades
9 Gems
10 China
11 Japan
12 Tibet
13 Earth Sciences
14 Pacific Spirits
15 Traveling the Pacific
16 Maori House
17 Eskimos and Northwest Coast Indians
18 Place for Wonder
19 Webber Resource Center
20 Webber Gallery
21 Plains Indians and Indians Before Columbus
22 Indians of the Woodlands & Prairies Pawnee Earth Lodge
23 Special Exhibits
24 Living Together
25 Mexico and Central America
26 South America
27 Stanley Field Hall
28 Nature Walk
29 North American Birds
30 World of Birds
31 World of Mammals
32 Tsavo Lions
33 Rice Wildlife Research Station
34 Mammals of Africa
35 Messages from the Wilderness
36 Mammals of Asia
37 Africa
38 Reptiles & Amphibians
39 Bird Habitats
40 What is an Animal?
41 Animal Biology
42 Egypt Tomb
43 Special Exhibits Gallery
44 Picnic in the Field-Deli
45 Insects
46 Inside Ancient Egypt
47 Education Department
48 James Simpson Theatre
49 Sea Mammals
50 McDonald's

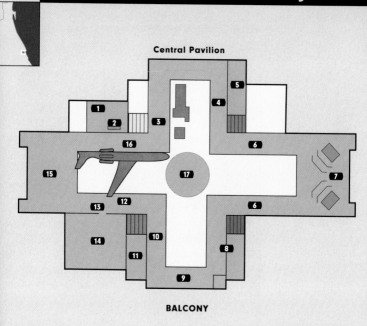

Central Pavilion

BALCONY

KEY
? Information
🚹 Restrooms
☎ Telephones

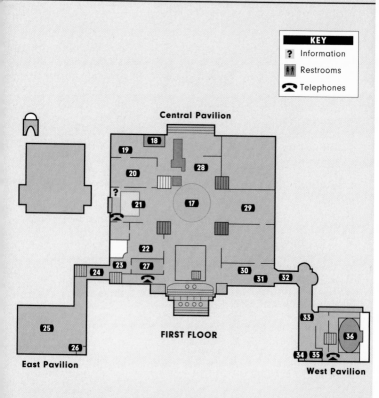

Central Pavilion

FIRST FLOOR

East Pavilion

West Pavilion

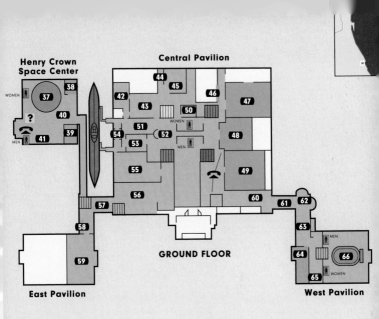

Henry Crown Space Center

WOMEN

Central Pavilion

MEN

GROUND FLOOR

MEN

WOMEN

East Pavilion

West Pavilion

Listed by Site Number

1 Homes
2 Kungsholm Puppets
3 Environmental Sciences
4 Regenstein Hall of Chemistry
5 MSI Presents LEGO MindStorms
6 Grainger Hall of Basic Science
7 Science Demonstrations
8 AIDS: The War Within
9 Brain
10 Sickle Cell
11 Heart
12 Flight 727 Observation Deck
13 Junior Achievement Business Hall of Fame
14 Kids' Starway
15 Designed to Fly
16 Take Flight
17 Rotunda
18 Finnigan's Ice Cream Parlor
19 Yesterday's Main Street

20 Auto Gallery
21 Railway Gallery
22 Food for Life
23 Delivering the Mail
24 Spaceport
25 Navy: Technology at Sea
26 Flight Simulators
27 Museum Shop
28 Coal Mine
29 Beyond Numbers
30 Communications
31 The World-Live! Demonstration
32 Whispering Gallery
33 Imaging
34 Mystery at the Museum
35 Virtual Reality
36 Auditorium
37 Omnimax Theater
38 Astro Cafe
39 Galaxy Shop
40 Apollo 8
41 Space Shuttle
42 Plumbing
43 Energy Lab

44 Yesterday's Firefighters
45 Fairy Castle
46 Vending Machines
47 Pizza Hut
48 Century Room
49 Cafe Spectrum
50 Science Theater
51 Biology Annex: Prenatal Development
52 Science in the News
53 LEGO Launch Pad
54 U-505 Submarine
55 Idea Factory
56 Circus
57 Eye Spy
58 USS Tag-It Shop
59 Alvin Submersible Craft
60 Ships Through the Ages
61 Racing Cars
62 Solar Racer
63 Dolls
64 Student Dining Area
65 Group Center
66 Little Theater

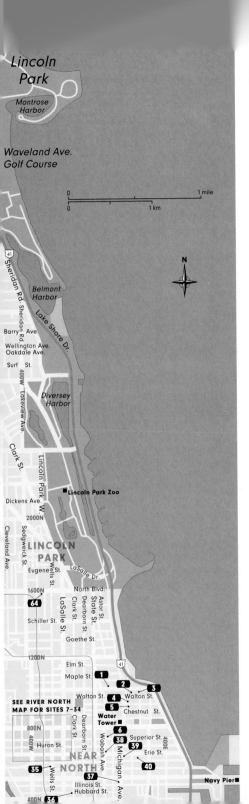

**Listed by
Site Number**

1 Aaron
  Galleries

2 Galleries
  Maurice Sternberg

3 Wally Findlay
  Galleries, Inc.

4 Lallak + Tom

5 Richard Gray
  Gallery

5 Alan Koppel Gallery

6 Kenneth Probst
  Galleries

35 Spencer Weisz
  Galleries, Ltd

36 Anchor Graphics

37 Kenyon
  Oppenheimer, Inc.

38 R H Love Galleries

39 R S Johnson Fine Art

39 Worthington Gallery

40 Campanile
  Galleries, Inc.

41 Kelmscott
  Gallery

42 Peter Jones

43 Schabes
  Gallery

44 Fourth World
  Artisans

45 Lill Street Gallery

46 Intuit

59 David Leonardis
  Gallery

60 Wood Street Gallery

61 Workshop Print
  Gallery

62 Cortland-Leyton
  Gallery

63 Artemesia

64 Eastwick Art Gallery

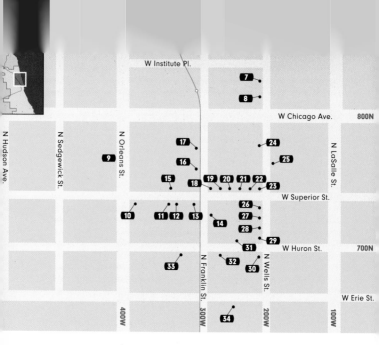

River North Detail Listed by Site Number

7 Bianca Pilat Contemporary Art

8 Orca Aart Gallery

9 Carol Ehler

10 Phyllis Kind Gallery

11 Printworks Gallery

11 Sonia Zaks

12 Fassbender Gallery

13 Lydon Fine Art, Inc

14 Robert Henry Adams Fine Art

15 Belloc Lowndes Fine Art

15 Catherine Edelman Gallery

15 Gallery A Inc.

15 Judy A Saslow Gallery

15 Lyons-Wier Gallery

16 Mary Bell Gallery

17 Lineage Gallery

17 Eastern Gallery

17 Byron Roche

18 G R N'Namdi

18 I space

18 Nicole Gallery

18 Marx-Saunders Gallery, Ltd

18 Satori Fine Art

18 Schneider Gallery

18 Vale Craft Gallery

19 Gruen Galleries

20 Galeria Amalia Mahoney

20 Habatat Galleries

21 Ann Nathan Gallery

22 Perimeter Gallery

23 Carl Hammer Gallery

24 Portals, Ltd

25 Roy Boyd Gallery

26 Jean Albano Gallery

26 Kass/Meridian

26 NIU Gallery

26 Maya Polsky Gallery

27 Primitive Art Works

28 Gwenda Jay Gallery

29 Mongerson Wunderlich Galleries

30 R Duane Reed Gallery

31 Douglas Dawson Gallery

32 Aldo Castillo Gallery

33 Zolla/Lieberman Gallery

34 Jan Cicero Gallery

Art Galleries Listed Alphabetically

Aaron Galleries, 1.
50 E Oak St ☎ 943-0660

Alan Koppel Gallery, 5.
875 N Michigan Ave ☎ 640-0730

Aldo Castillo Gallery, 32.
233 W Huron St ☎ 337-2536

Anchor Graphics, 36.
119 W Hubbard St ☎ 595-9598

Ann Nathan Gallery, 22.
218 W Superior St ☎ 664-6622

Artemisia, 63.
700 N Carpenter St ☎ 226-7323

Belloc Lowndes Fine Art, 15.
300 W Superior St ☎ 573-1157

Beret International Gallery, 53.
1550 N Milwaukee Ave
☎ 773/489-6518

Bianca Pilat Contemporary Art, 7.
814 N Franklin St ☎ 751-1470

Listed Alphabetically (cont.)

Byron Roche, 17.
750 N Franklin St ☎ 654-0144

Campanile Galleries, Inc, 40. 218
E Ontario St ☎ 642-3869

Carl Hammer Gallery, 23.
200 W Superior St ☎ 266-8512

Carol Ehler, 9.
750 N Orleans St ☎ 642-8611

Catherine Edelman Gallery, 15.
300 W Superior St ☎ 266-2350

Chicago Project Room, 57.
1464 N Milwaukee Ave
☎ 773/862-9209

Collage Gallery, 56.
1520 N Milwaukee Ave
☎ 773/252-2562

Cortland-Leyton Gallery, 62.
815 N Milwaukee Ave ☎ 773/733-2781

Creative Artists Saloon, 55.
1561 N Milwaukee Ave
☎ 773/278-7784

David Leonardis Gallery, 59.
1352 N Paulina St ☎ 773/278-3058

Douglas Dawson Gallery, 31.
222 W Huron St ☎ 751-1961

Eastern Gallery, 17.
750 N Franklin St ☎ 280-0787

Eastwick Art Gallery, 64.
245 W North Ave ☎ 773/440-2322

Fassbender Gallery, 12.
309 W Superior St ☎ 951-5979

Fourth World Artisans, 44.
3440 N Southport Ave
☎ 773/404-5200

Galeria Amalia Mahoney, 20.
222 W Superior St ☎ 943-9880

Galleries Maurice Sternberg, 2.
140 E Walton St ☎ 642-1700

Gallery A, Inc., 15.
300 W Superior St ☎ 280-4500

Gallery 203, 54. 1579 N Milwaukee
Ave ☎ 773/252-1952

G R N'Namdi Gallery, 18.
230 W Huron St ☎ 587-8262

Gruen Galleries, 19.
226 W Superior St ☎ 337-6262

Gwenda Jay Gallery, 28.
704 W Wells St ☎ 664-3406

Habatat Galleries, 20.
222 W Superior St ☎ 440-0288

I space, 18.
230 W Superior St ☎ 587-9976

Idao, 51.
1616 N Damen Ave ☎ 773/784-2559

InsideART, 58.
1651 W North Ave ☎ 773/772-4416

**Intuit: The Center for
Intuitive and Outsider Art, 46.**
1926 N Halsted St ☎ 773/929-7122

Jan Cicero Gallery, 34.
221 W Erie St ☎ 440-1904

Jean Albano Gallery, 26.
215 W Superior St ☎ 440-0770

Judy A Saslow Gallery, 15.
300 W Superior St ☎ 943-0530

Kass/Meridian, 26.
215 W Superior St ☎ 266-5999

Kelmscott Gallery, 41.
4611 N Lincoln Ave ☎ 773/784-2559

Kenneth Probst Galleries, 6.
46 E Superior St ☎ 440-1991

Kenyon Oppenheimer, Inc., 37.
410 N Michigan Ave ☎ 642-5300

Lallak + Tom, 4.
919 N Michigan Ave ☎ 943-7701

Lill Street Gallery, 45.
1021 W Lill Ave ☎ 773/477-6185

Lineage Gallery, 17.
750 N Franklin St ☎ 944-1960

Lydon Fine Art, Inc., 13.
301 W Superior St ☎ 943-1133

Lyons-Wier Gallery, 15.
300 W Superior St ☎ 654-0600

Marx-Saunders Gallery, Ltd., 18.
230 W Superior St ☎ 573-1400

Mary Bell Galleries, 16.
740 N Franklin St ☎ 642-0202

Maya Polsky Gallery, 26.
215 W Superior St ☎ 440-0055

**Mongerson Wunderlich Galleries,
29.** 702 N Wells St ☎ 943-2354

Nicole Gallery, 18.
230 W Huron St ☎ 787-7716

NIU Gallery, 26.
215 W Superior St ☎ 642-6010

Oh Boy!, 47.
2060 N Damen Ave ☎ 773/772-0101

Orca Aart Gallery, 8.
812 N Franklin St ☎ 280-4975

Perimeter Gallery, 22.
210 W Superior St ☎ 266-9473

Peter Jones, 42.
1806 W Cuyler Ave ☎ 773/472-6725

Phyllis Kind Gallery, 10.
313 W Superior St ☎ 642-6302

Portals, Ltd., 24.
742 N Wells St ☎ 642-1066

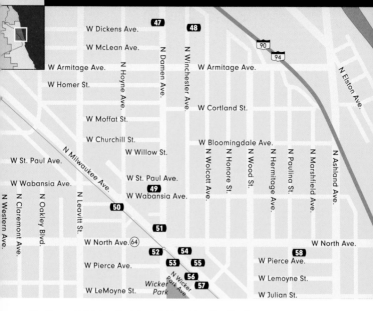

Bucktown & Wicker Park Detail Listed by Site Number

47 Oh Boy!

48 Thomas McCormick

49 Portia Gallery

50 Yello Gallery

51 Idao

52 Ten in One Gallery

53 Beret International Gallery

54 Gallery 203

55 Creative Artists Salon

56 Collage Gallery

57 Chicago Project Room

58 InsideArt

Listed Alphabetically

Portia Gallery, 49.
1702 N Damen Ave ☎ 773/862–1700

Primitve Art Works, 27.
706 N Wells St ☎ 943–3770

Printworks Gallery, 11.
311 W Superior St ☎ 664–9407

R Duane Reed Gallery, 30.
215 W Huron St ☎ 932–9828

R H Love Galleries, 38.
40 E Erie St ☎ 640–1300

R.S. Johnson Fine Art, 39.
645 N Michigan Ave ☎ 943–1661

Richard Gray Gallery, 5.
875 N Michigan Ave ☎ 642–8877

Robert Henry Adams Fine Art, 14.
715 N Franklin St ☎ 642–8700

Roy Boyd Gallery, 25.
739 N Wells St ☎ 642–1606

Satori Fine Art, 18.
230 W Superior St ☎ 751–1883

Schabes Gallery, 43.
3810 N Clark St ☎ 773/281–5550

Schneider Gallery, 18.
230 W Superior St ☎ 988–4033

Sonia Zaks, 11.
311 W Superior St ☎ 943–8440

Spencer Weisz Galleries, Ltd. 35.
214 W Ohio St ☎ 527–9420

Ten in One Gallery, 52.
1542 N Damen Ave ☎ 773/486–5820

Thomas McCormick Works of Art, 48.
2055 N Winchester Ave
☎ 773/227–0440

Vale Craft Gallery, 18.
230 W Superior St ☎ 337–3525

Wally Findlay Galleries, Inc., 3.
188 E Walton St ☎ 649–1500

Wood Street Gallery, 60.
1239 N Wood St ☎ 773/227–3306

Workshop Print Gallery, 61.
1101 N Paulina St ☎ 773/235–3712

Worthington Gallery, 39.
645 N Michigan Ave ☎ 266–2424

Yello Gallery, 50.
1630 N Milwaukee Ave
☎ 773/235–9731

Zolla/Lieberman Gallery, 33.
325 W Huron St ☎ 944–1990

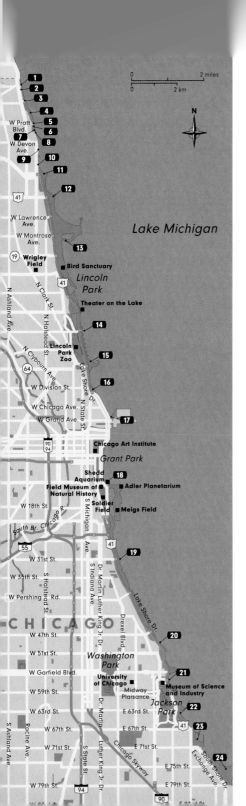

	0		2 miles
	0		2 km

N

Lake Michigan

W Pratt Blvd.
W Devon Ave.

W Lawrence Ave.
W Montrose Ave.

41

Wrigley Field

Bird Sanctuary

Lincoln Park

N Clark St.

N Halsted St.

N Ashland Ave.

Theater on the Lake

N Clybourn Ave.

64

Lincoln Park Zoo

W Division St.

W Chicago Ave.

W Grand Ave.

Lake Shore Dr.

N State St.

90
94

Chicago Art Institute

Grant Park

Shedd Aquarium

Field Museum of Natural History

Adler Planetarium

S Michigan Ave.

Soldier Field

Meigs Field

W 18th St.

South Br. Chicago R.

55

W 31st St.

W 35th St.

S Holsted St.

W Pershing Rd.

C H I C A G O

W 47th St.

W 51st St.

W Garfield Blvd.

S Indiana Ave.

Dr. Martin Luther King Jr. Dr.

Drexel Blvd.

Washington Park

University of Chicago

Midway Plaisance

Museum of Science and Industry

Jackson Park

W 59th St.

W 63rd St.

E 63rd St.

Dr. Martin Luther King Jr. Dr.

41

W 67th St.

E 67th St.

S State St.

S Ashland Ave.

Racine Ave.

Chicago Skyway

W 71st St.

E 71st St.

South Shore Dr.

Exchange Ave.

W 79th St.

E 75th St.

E 79th St.

94

90

Listed by Site Number

1 Fargo Ave Park & Beach
2 Jarvis Ave Park & Beach
3 Leone Park & Beach
4 Loyola Beach
5 Pratt Blvd Park & Beach
6 Columbia Ave Park & Beach
7 North Shore Ave Park & Beach
8 Hartigan Park & Beach
9 Berger Park & Beach
10 Lane Park & Beach
11 Osterman Beach
12 Foster Ave Beach
13 Montrose-Wilson Beach
14 Fullerton Beach
15 North Ave Beach
16 Oak St Beach
17 Ohio St Beach
18 12th St Beach
19 31st St Beach
20 49th St Beach
21 57th St Beach
22 64th St Beach
23 South Shore Country Club Beach
24 Rainbow Beach

Pottawattomie Park
Rogers Park
Rogers Ave. Park
Jarvis Ave. Park
Touhy Park
W Touhy Ave.
Lerner Park
Indian Boundary Park
Loyola Park
Chippewa Park
Warren Park
W Pratt Blvd.
Pratt Blvd. Park
Hartigan Park
W Devon Ave.
Loyola U
Green Briar Park
Berger Park
Lane Park
W Peterson St.
Mather Park
Senn Park
Legion Park
14
W Foster St.
Winnemac Park
River Park
Welles Park
Lincoln Park
41
W Lawrence Ave.
Clarendon Park
N Lincoln Ave.
W Montrose Ave.
Horner Park
19
McFetridge Athletic Center
Wrigley Field
Chicago Corinthian Yacht Club
Waveland Golf Course
W Addison Ave.
N Damen Ave.
N Ashland Ave.
N Clark St.
Bird Sanctuary
Chicago Yacht Club
W Belmont Ave.
Hamlin Park
Diversey Driving Range
Wrightwood Park
N Halstead Ave.
Diversey Yacht Club
Palmer Square
Holstein Park
Oz Park
Lincoln Park Zoo
Lincoln Park
N California Ave.
N Clybourn Ave.
Lake Michigan
N Western Ave.
64
Wicker Park
Clemente Park
Pulaski Park
Stanton
Schiller Park
Lake Shore Park
Humboldt Park
Eckhart Park
Seward Park
W Division St.
Smith Field Park
W Chicago Ave.
Washington Sq. Park
N State St.
W Grand Ave.
Bickerdike Sq. Park
Olive Park
Navy Pier Park
Union Park
90
94
MetroGolf Illinois Center
Washington Blvd.
W Madison St.
Columbia Yacht Club/
Chicago Yacht Club
United Center
Garibaldi Park
Arrigo Park
UIC
Altgeld Park
Sheridan Park
Grant Park
CHICAGO
Field Museum
Shedd Aquarium
Douglas Park
Addams Park
Dvorak Park
Adler Planetarium
Burnham Harbor Yacht Club
W 18th St.
Harrison Park
S Blue Island Ave.
Soldier Field
Northerly Island
W Cermak Rd.
S Michigan Ave.
South Br.
Chicago R.
55
McGuane Park
Williams Park
41
Dunbar Park
W 31st St.
S Indiana Ave.
Lake Meadows Park
Groveland Park
Woodland Park
Hoyne Park
W 35th St.
Armour Park
Dr. Martin Luther King Jr. Dr.
Ellis Park
Stevenson Expwy.
S Halstead Ave.
Comiskey Park
Madden Park
Burnham Park
McKinley Park
W Pershing Rd.
Stateway Park
Kelly Park
Davis Sq. Park
Drexel Blvd.
Kenwood Park
S Archer Ave.
Fuller Park
Harold Washington Park
S Kedzie Ave.
Cornell Sq. Park
W 47th St.
Taylor Park
S California Ave.
W 51st St.
Sherman Park
Washington Park
Nichols Park
W Garfield Blvd.
Sherwood Park
University of Chicago
Museum of Science and Industry
Gage Park
Hermitage Park
W 59th St.
Midway Plaisance
Jackson Park
Lindblom Park
Dr. Martin Luther King Jr. Dr.
Marquette Park
W 63rd St.
Ogden Park
E 63rd St.
Jackson Park Yacht Club/
Shore Yacht Club
S Western Ave.
S Damen Ave.
S Ashland Ave.
Racine Ave.
W 67th St.
94
E 67th St.
South Shore Cultural Center
S Kedzie Ave.
W 71st St.
S State
E 71st St.
Hodes Park
90
Rainbow Park
Hamilton

KEY

Beaches	
Bike paths	
Fishing	
Golf Courses	
Marinas	
Swimming Pools	
Tennis Courts	

0 ——— 2 miles
0 ——— 2 km

N

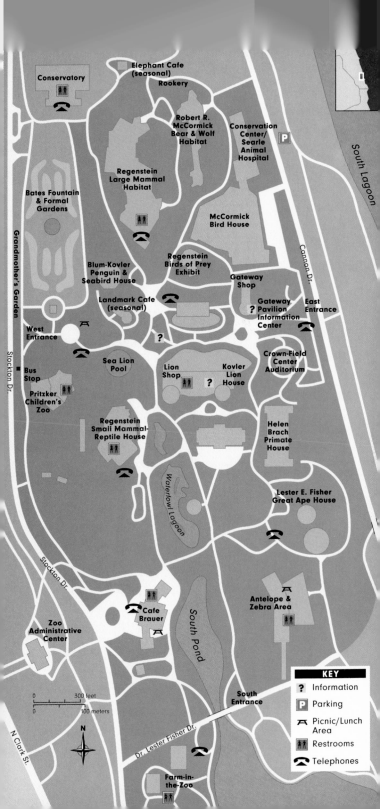

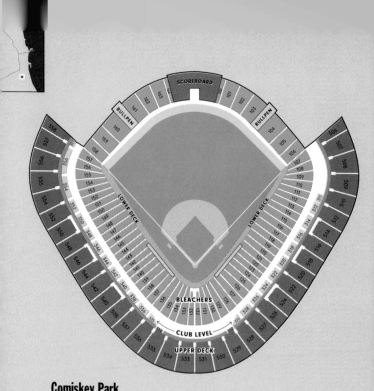

Comiskey Park

Wrigley Field

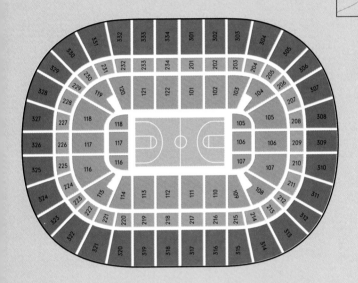

United Center

Soldier Field

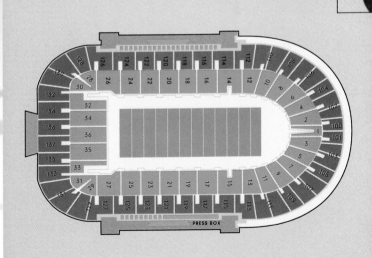

PRESS BOX

Sportsman's CC
Northbrook
Dundee Rd.
Glencoe GC
94
Green Bay Rd.
Glencoe
Anetsberger GC
Tower Rd.
Willow Rd.
43
Winnetka GC
Winnetka
Northfield
Glenview Naval Air Station GC
Glenview
Wilmette GC
Kenilworth
Lake Ave.
Peter Jans GC
21
Glenview Rd.
58
Glenview Park District GC
Golf
Weber Park GC
Wilmette
41
Morton Grove
Chick Evans GC
Evanston
14
Niles
Dempster St.
58
Skokie
Tam-O-Shanter GC
94
Lincolnwood
Touhy Ave.
Robert Black GC
43
14
Caldwell GC
Devon Ave.
Park Ridge
90
Peterson Ave.
14
72
Foster Ave.
41
Lake Michigan
Lawrence Ave.
19
Lake Shore Dr.
Norridge
Irving Park Rd.
90
94
Milwaukee Ave.
Marovitz/ Waveland GC
Indian Boundary GC
Addison St.
50
Belmont Ave.
Lincoln Ave.
Diversey Driving Range
Elmwood Park
Fullerton Ave.
Western Ave.
41
Park
River Forest
North Ave.
64
Oak Park
Columbus Park GC
Maywood
43
Washington Blvd
MetroGolf/ Illinois Center
290
Forest Park
50
Roosevelt Rd
38
Cicero
Ogden Ave.
Berwyn
Riverside
Brookfield
55
Archer Ave.
90
94
20
34
Stickney
Dr. M.L.King Jr. Dr.
41
Lyons
CHICAGO
N
Midway Airport
Garfield Blvd.
Summit
171
Marquette Park GC
Western Ave.
Halsted St.
Ashland Ave.
Jackson Park GC
Bedford Park
Pulaski Rd.
90
South Shore GC
79th St.
Chicago Skyway
Bridgeview
Burbank
50
Lake Shore Dr.
Hickory Hills
43
87th St.
Evergreen CC
95th St.
12
20
Oak Lawn
Evergreen Park
95th St.
Hickory Hills CC
45
Stony Creek GC
103rd St.
Harborside International GC
Palos Hills CC
COOK COUNTY
111th St.
57
Stony Island Ave.
Worth
The Meadows GC
Torrence Ave.
83
Fountain Hills GC
Pipe of Peace GC
94
Rd.
50
127th St.
Palos GC
Oak Hills GC
Westgate Valley CC
Palos Heights
Blue Island
Riverdale
Dolton
Burnham Woods GC
Calumet City
7
Silver Lake GC
Midlothian
Cicero Ave.
294
INDIANA
ILLINOIS

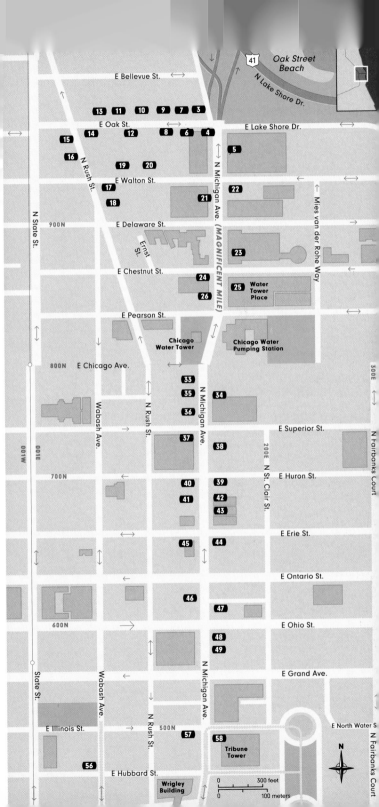

Listed by Site Number

NEAR NORTH

1 Barbara's Bookstore
2 Mr Kite's Gold Coast Confectionery
3 Ultimo
4 Giorgio Armani
5 Chanel
6 Ann Taylor
7 Hermès
8 Gianni Versace
9 Elements
10 Hino & Malee
11 Jil Sander
12 CP Shades
13 MAC Cosmetics
14 Barneys New York
15 Tender Buttons
16 Hear Music
17 Diesel
18 Children in Paradise
19 agnès b
20 Battaglia
21 Bloomingdales
21 J Crew
22 Mark Shale
23 Chicago Architecture Foundation
23 Paul Stuart
24 Escada
24 FAO Schwarz
25 Water Tower Place
25 Rizzoli International Bookstore
25 Marshall Field & Co
25 Lord & Taylor
26 Borders Books & Music
27 Paper Source
28 Alcala's Western Wear
29 Pearl
30 Michael FitzSimmons
31 Fly-By-Nite
32 June Blaker
33 Pottery Barn
34 Neiman Marcus
35 Banana Republic
36 Tiffany & Co
37 Saks Fifth Avenue
38 Brooks Brothers
39 Cole Haan
40 The Limited

41 Joan & David
42 NikeTown
43 Sony
44 Ferragamo
45 Crate & Barrel
46 Original Levi's Store
46 Eddie Bauer
47 Bigsby & Kruthers
48 Timberland
49 Forgotten Woman
50 SportMart
51 Mario Villa
52 Rita Bucheit, Ltd
53 Antiques Center at Kinzie Square
54 Sawbridge Studios
55 Golden Triangle
56 Jazz Record Mart
57 Rand McNally Map & Travel Store
58 Hammacher Schlemmer
59 The Kite Harbor

DOWNTOWN

60 Illinois Artisans Shop
61 Marshall Field & Co
62 B Dalton
63 Crate & Barrel
64 Syd Jerome
65 Altman's Men's Shoes and Boots
66 Carson Pirie Scott & Co
67 Iwan Ries & Co.
68 Charrette
69 Crown Books
70 Crown Books
71 Brooks Brothers
72 B Dalton
73 Leonidas Chicago
74 ABC Delicious
75 E B Collington Ltd
76 The Library Store
77 Prairie Avenue Bookshop
78 Afrocentric Bookstore
79 Carl Fischer
80 Central Camera
81 Tower Records/ Videos/Books
82 Chicago Architecture Foundation
83 Rain Dog Books

Listed Alphabetically

NEAR NORTH

agnès b, 19. 46 E Walton St
☎ 642-7483. Womenswear

Alcala's Western Wear, 28.
1733 W Chicago Ave ☎ 226-0152

Ann Taylor, 6. 103 E Oak St
☎ 943-5411. Womenswear

**Antiques Center at Kinzie Square,
53.** 220 W Kinzie St ☎ 464-1946

Banana Republic, 35. 744 N.
Michigan Ave ☎ 642-0020. Clothing

Barbara's Bookstore, 1.
1350 N Wells St ☎ 642-5044

Barneys New York, 14. 25 E Oak St
☎ 587-1700. Clothing

Battaglia, 20. 70 E Walton St
☎ 787-3237. Shoes

Bigsby & Kruthers, 47. 605 N.
Michigan Ave ☎ 397-0430.
Menswear

Bloomingdales, 21. 900 N. Michigan
Ave ☎ 440-4596. Department Store

Borders Books & Music, 26.
830 N. Michigan Ave ☎ 573-0564

Brooks Brothers, 38. 713 N. Michigan
Ave ☎ 915-0060. Clothing

Chanel, 5. 935 N. Michigan Ave
☎ 787-5500. Womenswear

**Chicago Architecture Foundation,
23.** 875 N Michigan Ave ☎ 751-1380.
Architecture Books/Crafts

Children in Paradise, 18. 909 N Rush
St ☎ 851-9437. Children's Books

Cole Haan, 39. 673 N Michigan Ave
☎ 642-8995. Shoes

CP Shades, 12. 49 E Oak St
☎ 337-0170. Womenswear

Crate & Barrel, 45. 646 N Michigan
Ave ☎ 787-5900. Housewares

Diesel, 17. 923 N Rush St ☎ 255-0157.
Clothing

Eddie Bauer, 46. 600 N Michigan
Ave ☎ 951-8484. Clothing

Elements, 9. 102 E Oak St
☎ 642-6574. Home Furnishings

Escada, 24. 840 N Michigan Ave
☎ 915-0500. Womenswear

FAO Schwarz, 24. 840 N Michigan
Ave ☎ 587-5000. Toys

Ferragamo, 44. 645 N Michigan Ave
☎ 397-0464. Shoes

Fly-By-Nite, 31. 714 N Wells St
☎ 664-8136. Antiques

Forgotten Woman, 49. 535 N
Michigan Ave ☎ 329-0885.
Larger-size Womenswear

Gianni Versace, 8. 101 E Oak St
☎ 337-1111. Clothing

Giorgio Armani, 4. 113 E Oak St
☎ 751-2244. Clothing

The Golden Triangle, 55. 72 W
Hubbard ☎ 755-1266. Asian Antiques

Hammacher Schlemmer, 58. 445 N
Michigan Ave ☎ 527-9100. Gadgets

Hear Music, 16. 932 N Rush St
☎ 951-0242. Records

Hermès of Paris, 7. 110 E Oak St
☎ 787-8175. Clothing

Hino & Malee, 10. 50 E Oak St
☎ 664-7475. Womenswear

J Crew, 21. 900 N Michigan Ave
☎ 751-2739. Clothing

Jazz Record Mart, 56. 444 N
Wabash Ave ☎ 222-1467

Jil Sander, 11. 48 E Oak St
☎ 335-0006. Womenswear

Joan & David, 41. 670 N Michigan
Ave ☎ 482-8585. Shoes

June Blaker, 32. 200 W Superior St
☎ 751-9220. Clothing

The Kite Harbor, 59. 435 E Illinois St
☎ 321-5483

The Limited, 40. 676 N Michigan Ave
☎ 944-5770. Womenswear

Lord & Taylor, 25. 835 N Michigan
Ave ☎ 787-7400. Department Store

MAC Cosmetics, 13. 40 E Oak St
☎ 951-7310

Mario Villa, 51. 500 N Wells St
☎ 923-0993. Art Furniture

Mark Shale, 22. 919 N Michigan Ave
☎ 440-0720. Clothing

Marshall Field & Co, 25.
835 N Michigan Ave ☎ 335-7700.
Department Store

**Michael FitzSimmons Decorative
Arts, 30.** 311 W Superior St
☎ 787-0496. Antiques

**Mr. Kite's Gold Coast
Confectionery, 2.** 1153 N State St
☎ 664-7270. Chocolates

Neiman Marcus, 34. 737 N Michigan
Ave ☎ 642-5900. Department Store

NikeTown, 42. 669 N Michigan Ave
☎ 642-6363. Sporting Goods

Listed Alphabetically

Original Levi's Store, 46.
600 N Michigan Ave
☎ 642-9613. Jeans

Paper Source, 27. 232 W Chicago
Ave ☎ 337-0798. Stationary

Paul Stuart, 23. 875 N Michigan Ave
☎ 640-2650. Menswear

Pearl, 29. 225 W Chicago Ave
☎ 915-0200. Art Supplies

Pottery Barn, 33.
734 N Michigan Ave ☎ 587-9602.
Housewares

**Rand McNally Map & Travel Store,
57.** 444 N Michigan Ave ☎ 321-1751

Rita Bucheit, Ltd. 52. 449 N Wells
☎ 527-4080. Antiques

**Rizzoli International Bookstore and
Gallery, 25.** 835 N Michigan Ave
☎ 642-3500

Saks Fifth Avenue, 37.
700 N Michigan Ave ☎ 944-6500.
Department Store

Sawbridge Studios, 54.
406 N Clark St ☎ 828-0055.
Furniture/Crafts

**Sony Gallery of Consumer
Electronics, 43.** 663 N Michigan Ave
☎ 943-0817

SportMart, 50. 650 N LaSalle
☎ 337-6151. Sporting Goods

Tender Buttons, 15. 946 N Rush St
☎ 337-7033. Buttons

Tiffany & Co., 36.
730 N Michigan Ave ☎ 944-7500.
Jewelery

Timberland, 48. 543 N Michigan Ave
☎ 494-0171. Shoes/Boots

Ultimo, 3. 114 E Oak St ☎ 787-1171.
Clothing

Water Tower Place, 25.
835 N Michigan Ave ☎ 440-3166.
Shopping Center

DOWNTOWN

ABC Delicious, 74. 316 S Dearborn St
☎ 427-7766. Chocolates

Afrocentric Bookstore, 78. 333 S
State St ☎ 939-1956

**Altman's Men's Shoes and Boots,
65.** 120 W Monroe St ☎ 332-0667

B Dalton Booksellers, 62.
129 N Wabash Ave ☎ 236-7615

B Dalton Booksellers, 72.
175 W Jackson Blvd ☎ 922-5219

Brooks Brothers, 71. 209 S LaSalle St
☎ 263-0100. Menswear

Carl Fischer, 79. 312 S Wabash Ave
☎ 427-6652. Sheet Music

Carson Pirie Scott & Co., 66.
1 S State St ☎ 641-7000. Dept. Store

Central Camera, 80.
230 S Wabash Ave ☎ 427-5580

Charrette, 68.
23 S Wabash Ave ☎ 782-5737.
Art Supplies

**Chicago Architecture Foundation,
82.** 224 S Michigan Ave ☎ 922-3432.
Architecture Books/Crafts

Crate & Barrel, 63.
101 N Wabash Ave ☎ 372-0100.
Housewares

Crown Books, 69. 105 S Wabash Ave
☎ 782-7667

Crown Books, 70. 144 S Clark St
☎ 857-0613

E B Collington Ltd., 75.
318 S Dearborn St ☎ 431-1888.
Fountain Pens

Illinois Artisans Shop, 60.
100 W Randolph St ☎ 814-5321.
Crafts

Iwan Ries & Co, 67.
19 S Wabash Ave ☎ 372-1306.
Cigars/Pipes

Leonidas Chicago, 73.
231 S LaSalle St ☎ 251-8850.
Chocolates

The Library Store, 76. 400 S State St
☎ 747-4130. Stationary/Crafts

Marshall Field & Co, 61.
111 N State St ☎ 781-1000.
Department Store

Prairie Avenue Bookshop, 77.
418 S Wabash Ave ☎ 922-8311.
Architecture Books

Rain Dog Books, 83.
404 S Michigan Ave ☎ 922-1200.
Antiquarian Books

Syd Jerome, 64. 2 N LaSalle St
☎ 346-0333. Menswear

Tower Records/Videos/Books, 81.
214 S Wabash Ave ☎ 663-0660

Listed by Site Number

1   Swedish Bakery
2   Women & Children First
3   Home Bodies
4   Flashy Trash
5   Chicago Antique Center
6   The Good Old Days
7   Danger City
8   Lincoln Antique Mall
9   Uncle Fun
10 Bittersweet
11 The Stars Our Destination
12 Aiko's Art Materials
13 Windward Sports
14 Europa Books

15 Unabridged Bookstore
16 Reckless Records
17 Toyscape
18 Crown Books
19 Borders Books and Music
20 Barnes & Noble
21 Raymond Hudd, Inc.
22 Tower Records/ Videos/Books
23 Saturday's Child
24 Arete
25 Vivante Chocolatier
26 Tabula Tua
27 Bread with Appeal
28 Ancient Echoes

29 Active Endeavors
30 Coffee and Tea Exchange
31 Isis on Armitage
32 Mayet Bead Design
32 Renaissance Buttons
33 Cynthia Rowley
34 Art Effect
36 Land's End Outlet
37 Saffron
38 Cielo Vivo
39 EmbeLezar
40 Eclectic Junction
41 Pop Era
42 Green Acres
43 Quimby's

Listed Alphabetically

Active Endeavors, 29.
935 W Armitage Ave ☎ 773/281-8100.
Outdoor Clothes/Equipment

Aiko's Art Materials, 12.
3347 N Clark St ☎ 773/404-5600.
Handmade Paper

Ancient Echoes, 28.
1003 W Armitage Ave ☎ 773/880-1003
Crafts/Clothing

Arete, 24. 2154 N Halsted St
☎ 773/665-8708. Folk Art/Furniture

Art Effect, 34. 653 W Armitage Ave
☎ 664-0997. Womenswear

Barnes & Noble Booksellers, 20.
659 W Diversey Pkwy ☎ 773/871-9004

Bittersweet, 10. 1114 W Belmont Ave
☎ 773/929-1100. Bakery

Borders Books and Music, 19.
2817 N Clark St ☎ 773/935-3909

Bread with Appeal, 27. 1009 W
Armitage ☎ 773/244-2700. Bakery

Chicago Antique Center, 5.
3045 N Lincoln Ave ☎ 773/929-0200.
Antiques

Cielo Vivo, 38. 1866 N Damen Ave
☎ 773/276-8012. Antiques

Coffee and Tea Exchange, 30.
833 W Armitage Ave ☎ 773/929-6730

Crown Books, 35. 1714 N Sheffield
Ave ☎ 787-4370

Crown Books, 18. 801 W Diversey
Pkwy ☎ 773/327-1551

Cynthia Rowley, 33.
808 W Armitage Ave ☎ 773/528-6160.
Womenswear

Danger City, 7. 2129 W Belmont Ave
☎ 773/871-1420. Antiques

Eclectic Junction, 40.
1630 N Damen Ave ☎ 773/342-7865.
Crafts/Home Furnishings

EmbeLezar, 39. 1639 N Damen Ave
☎ 773/645-9705. Crafts/Home
Furnishings

Europa Books, 14. 3229 N Clark St
☎ 773/404-7313. Foreign-Language
Books

Flashy Trash, 4. 3524 N Halsted St
☎ 773/327-6900. Vintage Clothing

The Good Old Days, 6.
2138 W Belmont Ave ☎ 773/472-8837.
Antiques

Green Acres, 42. 1464 N Milwaukee
Ave ☎ 773/292-1998. Antiques

Home Bodies, 3. 3647 N
Halsted St ☎ 773/975-9393.
Home Furnishings

Isis on Armitage, 31. 823 W
Armitage Ave ☎ 773/665-7290.
Womenswear

Land's End Outlet, 36.
2121 N Clybourn Ave ☎ 773/281-0900.
Clothing

Lincoln Antique Mall, 8.
3141 N Lincoln Ave ☎ 773/244-1440.
Antiques

Mayet Bead Design, 32.
826 W Armitage Ave ☎ 773/868-0580

Pop Era, 41. 1941 W North Ave
☎ 773/384-4708. Movie Posters

Quimby's, 43. 1854 W North Ave
☎ 773/342-0910. Zines/Comics

Raymond Hudd, Inc, 21.
2545 N Clark St ☎ 773/477-1159. Hats

Reckless Records, 16.
3157 N Broadway ☎ 773/404-5080.
Vintage/New

Renaissance Buttons, 32.
826 W Armitage Ave ☎ 773/883-9508

Saffron, 37. 2064 N Damen Ave
☎ 773/486-7753. Womenswear.

Saturday's Child, 23.
2146 N. Halsted St ☎ 773/525-8697.
Toys

The Stars Our Destination, 11.
1021 W Belmont Ave ☎ 773/871-2722.
Science Fiction

Swedish Bakery, 1. 5348 N Clark St
☎ 773/561-8919

Tabula Tua, 26.
1015 W Armitage Ave ☎ 773/525-
3500. Tableware

Tower Records/Videos/Books, 22.
2301 N Clark St ☎ 773/477-5994

Toyscape, 17. 2911 N Broadway
☎ 773/665-7400. Toys

Unabridged Bookstore, 15.
3251 N Broadway ☎ 773/883-9119

Uncle Fun, 9. 1338 W Belmont Ave
☎ 773/477-8223. Toys

Vivante Chocolatier, 25.
1056 W Webster Ave ☎ 773/549-0123

Windward Sports, 13. 3317 N Clark
St ☎ 773/472-6868. Skate/Snow
Boarding

Women & Children First, 2.
5233 N Clark St ☎ 773/769-9299.
Lesbian/Feminist Books

Listed by Site Number

1	The Palm	6	Blackbird	11	Nick's Fishmarket
2	Primavera	7	Heaven on Seven	12	Vivere
2	Entre Nous	8	Trattoria No. 10	13	Voila!
3	Cusines	9	La Rosetta	14	The Berghoff
4	Catch 35	10	Rivers Euro-Ameri-can Bistro	15	Rhapsody
5	Shark Bar			16	Russian Tea Time

Listed Alphabetically

The Berghoff, 14. 17 W Adams St
☎ 427–3170. German. $–$$

Blackbird, 6. 619 W Randolph St
☎ 715–0708. New American. $$–$$$

Catch 35, 4. 35 W Wacker Dr
☎ 346–3500. Seafood. $$$–$$$$

Costa's, 23. 340 S Halsted St
☎ 263–9700. Greek. $$–$$$$

Cusines, 3. 1 W Wacker Dr
☎ 372–7200. Mediterranean. $$–$$$$

Entre Nous, 2. 200 N Columbus Dr
☎ 565–7997. French. $$–$$$$

Everest, 19. 440 S LaSalle St
☎ 663–8920. French. $$$$

Francesca's on Taylor, 25. 1400 W
Taylor St ☎ 829–2828. Italian. $–$$$

Gold Coast Dogs, 20. 225 S Canal St
☎ 258–8585. Hot Dogs. $

Heaven on Seven, 7. 111 N Wabash
Ave ☎ 263–6443. Cajun/Creole.
(Breakfast, lunch only) $

La Rosetta, 9. 70 W Madison St
☎ 332–9500. Italian. $$–$$$

Lou Mitchell's, 21. 565 W Jackson St
☎ 939–3111. Breakfast. $

Marché, 28. 833 W Randolph St
☎ 226–8399. French. $$–$$$$

New Rosebud Café, 26.
1500 W Taylor St ☎ 942–1117. Italian.
$$–$$$

Nick's Fishmarket, 11. 1 First National
Plaza ☎ 621–0200. Seafood. $$–$$$

One Sixtyblue, 29. 160 N Loomis St
☎ 850–0303. New American. $$–$$$

The Palm, 1. 323 E Wacker Dr
☎ 616–1000. Steakhouse. $$–$$$$

Parthenon, 22. 314 S Halsted St
☎ 726–2407. Greek. $–$$$

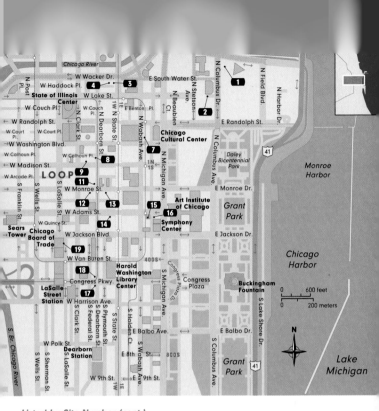

Listed by Site Number (cont.)

17 Printer's Row
18 Prairie
19 Everest
20 Gold Coast Dogs
21 Lou Mitchell's
22 Parthenon

23 Costa's
24 Tuscany
25 Francesca's on Taylor
26 New Rosebud Café
27 Wishbone

28 Marché
29 One Sixtyblue
30 Vivo
31 Red Light
32 Toque

Listed Alphabetically (cont.)

Prairie, 18. 500 S Dearborn St
☎ 663-1143. New American. $$–$$$$

Primavera, 2. 200 N Columbus Dr
☎ 565-6655. Italian. $$–$$$

Printer's Row, 17. 550 S Dearborn St
☎ 461-0780. New American. $$–$$$$

Red Light, 31. 820 W Randolph St
☎ 733-8880. Pan-Asian. $$–$$$

Rivers Euro-American Bistro, 10.
30 S Wacker Dr ☎ 559-1515.
American/French. $$–$$$

Rhapsody, 15. 77 E Adams St
☎ 786-9911. New American $$–$$$

Russian Tea Time, 16. 77 E Adams St
☎ 360-0000. Russian. $$–$$$$

Shark Bar, 5. 212 N Canal St
☎ 559-5057. Southern. $$–$$$

Toque, 32. 816 W Randolph St
☎ 666-1100. New American. $$–$$$

Trattoria No. 10, 8. 10 N Dearborn St
☎ 984-1718. Italian. $$–$$$

Tuscany, 24. 1014 W Taylor St
☎ 829-1990. Italian. $$–$$$

Vivere, 12. 71 W Monroe St
☎ 332-7005. Italian. $$–$$$

Vivo, 30. 838 W Randolph St
☎ 733-3379. Italian. $$–$$$

Voila!, 13. 33 W Monroe St
☎ 580-9500. Brasserie $$–$$$

Wishbone, 27. 1001 W Washington
☎ 850-2663. Southern. $$–$$$

$$$$ = over $50 $$$ = $30–$50 $$ = $20–$30 $ = under $20
Based on cost per person, excluding drinks, service, and 8.75% sales tax.

OLD TOWN

W Germania Pl.

W Burton Pl.

W Burton Pl.

E Burton Pl.

N Cleveland St.

N Hudson St.

N Sedgewick St.

N Orleans St.

N Park St.

N Wieland St.

N Wells St.

W Schiller St.

N LaSalle St.

N Clark St.

N Dearborn St.

N Parkway St.

N Astor St.

E Schiller St.

2

1

W Sullivan St.

W Evergreen St.

N Astor St.

N Banks St.

Ritchie Ct.

3

W Goethe St.

Schick Pl.

W Goethe St.

4

Goethe St.

N Stone St.

W Scott St.

E Scott St.

W Division St.

1200N

W Division St.

E Division St.

W Elm St.

Seward Park

W Elm St.

5

GOLD COAST

W Hobbie St.

W Hill St.

7

E Cedar St.

6

W Maple St.

E Bellevue St.

W Wendell St.

8

N Rush St.

E Oak St.

W Oak St.

W Oak St.

9

W Walton St.

W Walton St.

E Walton St.

N Hudson Ave.

N Wells St.

W Locust St.

Washington Square

E Delaware St.

W Delaware St.

19

W Delaware St.

N State St.

Ernst St.

W Chestnut St.

E Chestnut St.

W Chestnut St.

E Pearson St.

W Institute Pl.

RIVER NORTH

W Chicago Ave.

800N

W Chicago Ave.

E Chicago Ave.

20

E Chicago Ave.

N Hudson Ave.

N Sedgewick St.

N Orleans St.

N Franklin St.

21

W Superior St.

22

Clark St.

Dearborn St.

State St.

Wabash Ave.

N Rush St.

77

76

23

24

W Huron St.

74

NEAR NORTH

75

73

W Erie St.

72

400W

71

W Ontario St.

42

40

69

70

52

41

39

W Ohio St.

68

65
66

67

50

W Grand Ave.

58

51

49

64

59

57

N Kingsbury St.

61

W Illinois St.

48

47 **46**

54

43

63

W Hubbard St.

53

44

62

W Kinzie St.

60

400N

56

55

Wrigley Building

45

N Canal St.

Chicago River

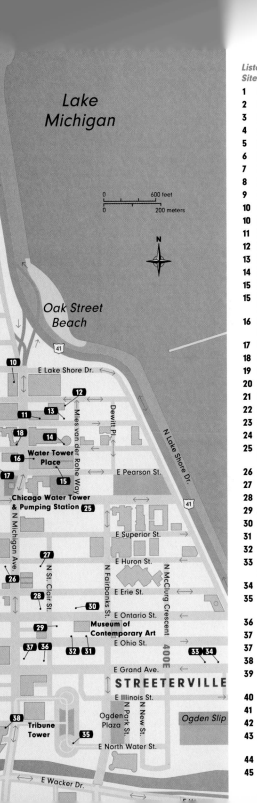

**Listed by
Site Number**

1 Kamehachi
2 Lucky Platter
3 The Pump Room
4 ¡Salpicón!
5 Tsunami
6 Big Bowl Café
7 Morton's of Chicago
8 Gibson's
9 Le Colonial
10 Café Spiagga
10 Spiagga
11 Seasons
12 Park Avenue Café
13 Mrs. Park's Tavern
14 The Saloon
15 Ritz-Carlton Café
15 Ritz-Carlton Dining Room
16 Signature Room at the 95th
17 Bistro 110
18 Iron Mike's Grill
19 Kiki's Bistro
20 Earth
21 Grapes
22 Café Iberico
23 Mango
24 Blackhawk Lounge
25 Eli's, the Place for Steak
26 Cielo
27 Avanzare
28 Hatsuhana
29 Capitol Grille
30 Les Nomades
31 Spruce
32 Dao
33 Joe's BeBob Café & Jazz Emporium
34 Riva
35 Mantuano Mediterranean Table
36 Boston Blackie's
37 Bandera
37 House of Hunan
38 Billy Goat Tavern
39 Heaven on Seven on Rush
40 Pizzeria Due
41 Pizzeria Uno
42 Papagus
43 Shaw's Crab House & Blue Crab Lounge
44 Gold Coast Dogs
45 Harry Caray's

Listed by Site Number (cont.)

- **46** Tucci Milan
- **47** Woo Lae Oak
- **48** Ruth's Chris Steak House
- **49** Ben Pao
- **50** Spago
- **51** Zinfandel
- **52** Hard Rock Café
- **53** Brasserie Jo
- **54** Frontera Grill
- **54** Topolobampo
- **55** Trattoria Parma
- **56** Mambo Grill
- **57** Gordon
- **58** Maggiano's Little Italy
- **59** Michael Jordan's
- **60** Havana
- **61** Coco Pazzo
- **62** Klay Oven
- **63** Hubbard Street Grill
- **64** Gene & Georgetti
- **65** Savannah's
- **66** Wishbone
- **67** Crofton on Wells
- **68** Cyrano's Bistrot & Wine Bar
- **69** Carson's Rib
- **70** Planet Hollywood
- **71** Ed Debevic's
- **72** Big Bowl Café
- **72** Wildfire
- **73** CoCoRo
- **74** Harvest on Huron
- **75** Hat Dance
- **76** Centro
- **77** Scoozi!

Listed Alphabetically

Avanzare, 27. 161 E Huron St ☎ 337-8056. Italian. $$-$$$

Bandera, 37. 535 N Michigan Ave ☎ 644-3524. American. $$

Ben Pao, 49. 52 W Illinois St ☎ 222-1888. Chinese. $-$$

Big Bowl Café, 6. 6 E Cedar St ☎ 640-8888. Pan-Asian. $

Big Bowl Café, 72. 159 1/2 W Erie St ☎ 787-8297. Pan-Asian. $

Billy Goat Tavern, 38. 430 N Michigan Ave ☎ 222-1525. Burgers. $

Bistro 110, 17. 110 E Pearson St ☎ 266-3110. French. $$-$$$

Blackhawk Lodge, 24. 41 E Superior St ☎ 280-4080. American. $$-$$$

Boston Blackie's, 36. 164 E Grand Ave ☎ 938-8700. Burgers. $

Brasserie Jo, 53. 59 W Hubbard St ☎ 595-0800. French. $$-$$$

Café Iberico, 22. 739 N LaSalle St ☎ 573-1510. Tapas. $$

Café Spiaggia, 10. 980 N Michigan Ave ☎ 280-2764. Italian. $$-$$$

Capital Grille, 29. 633 N St Clair St ☎ 337-9400. Steakhouse. $$-$$$

Carson's Ribs, 69. 612 N Wells St ☎ 280-9200. Ribs. $$

Centro, 76. 710 N Wells St ☎ 988-7775. Italian. $$-$$$

Cielo, 26. 676 N Michigan Ave ☎ 944-7676. Mediterranean. $$-$$$

Coco Pazzo, 61. 300 W Hubbard St ☎ 836-0900. Italian. $$$

CoCoRo, 73. 668 N Wells St ☎ 943-2220. Japanese. $$

Crofton on Wells, 67. 535 N Wells St ☎ 755-1790. New American. $$-$$$

Cyrano's Bistrot & Wine Bar, 68. 546 N Wells St ☎ 467-0546. French. $$

Dao, 32. 230 E Ohio St ☎ 337-0000. Thai. $

Earth, 20. 738 N Wells St ☎ 335-5475. American/Vegetarian.

Ed Debevic's, 71. 640 N Wells St ☎ 664-1707. American. $

Eli's the Place for Steaks, 25. 215 E Chicago Ave ☎ 642-1393. Steakhouse. $$-$$$

Frontera Grill, 54. 445 N Clark St ☎ 661-1434. Mexican. $-$$$

Gene & Georgetti, 64. 500 N Franklin St ☎ 527-3718. Steakhouse. $$-$$$

Gibson's, 8. 1028 N Rush St ☎ 266-8999. Steakhouse. $$$-$$$$

Gold Coast Dogs, 44. 418 N State St ☎ 527-1222. Hot Dogs. $

Gordon, 57. 500 N Clark St ☎ 467-9780. New American. $$$-$$$$

Grapes, 21. 733 N Wells St ☎ 943-4500. Mediterranean. $$

Hard Rock Café, 52. 63 W Ontario St ☎ 943-2252. American. $

Harry Caray's, 45. 33 W Kinzie St ☎ 465-9269. Italian/Steak. $$-$$$

Harvest on Huron, 74. 217 W Huron St ☎ 587-9600. New American. $$-$$$

Hat Dance, 75. 325 W Huron St ☎ 649-0066. Mexican. $$-$$$

Hatsuhana, 28. 160 E Ontario St ☎ 280-8808. Japanese. $$-$$$

Havana, 60. 230 W Kinzie St ☎ 595-0101. Cuban. $$-$$$

Heaven on Seven on Rush, 39. 600 N Michigan Ave ☎ 280-7774. Cajun/Creole. $$

House of Hunan, 37.
535 N Michigan Ave ☎ 329-9494.
Chinese. $$-$$$

Hubbard Street Grill, 63.
351 W Hubbard St ☎ 222-0770.
American. $$-$$$

Iron Mike's Grille, 18. 100 E Chestnut
St ☎ 587-8989. American. $$-$$$$

Joe's Be-Bop Café & Jazz Emporium, 33. Navy Pier, 600 E Grand Ave
☎ 595-5299. Ribs. $-$$$

Kamehachi, 1. 1400 N Wells St
☎ 664-3663. Japanese. $$

Kiki's Bistro, 19. 900 N Franklin St
☎ 335-5454. French. $$-$$$

Klay Oven, 62. 414 N Orleans St
☎ 527-3999. Indian. $$

Le Colonial, 9. 937 N Rush St
☎ 255-0088. Vietnamese. $$$

Les Nomades, 30. 222 E Ontario St
☎ 649-9010. French. $$$

Lucky Platter, 2. 1400 N Lake Shore
Dr ☎ 337-8130. Eclectic. $

Maggiano's Little Italy, 58. 516 N
Clark St ☎ 644-7700. Italian. $$-$$$

Mambo Grill, 56. 412 N Clark St
☎ 467-9797. Latin American. $$

Mango, 23. 712 N Clark St
☎ 337-5440. New American. $$-$$$

**Mantuano Mediterranean Table,
35.** 455 Cityfront Plaza ☎ 832-2600.
Mediterranean. $-$$$

Michael Jordan's, 59. 500 N LaSalle
St ☎ 644-3865. American. $$-$$$

Morton's of Chicago, 7.
1050 N State St ☎ 266-4820.
Steakhouse. $$$-$$$$

Mrs. Park's Tavern, 13.
198 E Delaware Pl ☎ 280-8882.
American. $$-$$$

Papagus, 42. 620 N State St
☎ 642-8450. Greek. $$-$$$

Park Avenue Café, 12.
199 E Walton Pl ☎ 944-4414. New
American. $$$-$$$$

Pizzeria Due, 40. 619 N Wabash Ave
☎ 943-2400. Pizza. $

Pizzeria Uno, 41. 29 E Ohio St
☎ 321-1000. Pizza. $

Planet Hollywood, 70. 633 N Wells
St ☎ 266-STAR. American. $-$$

The Pump Room, 3.
1301 N State Pkwy ☎ 266-0360.
American. $$$

Ritz-Carlton Café, 15. 160 E Pearson
St. ☎ 573-5160. American. $$-$$$

Ritz-Carlton Dining Room, 15.
160 E Pearson St ☎ 266-1000.
French. $$$-$$$$

Riva, 34. Navy Pier, 700 E Grand Ave
☎ 644-7482. Seafood. $$-$$$

Ruth's Chris Steak House, 48.
431 N Dearborn St ☎ 321-2725.
Steakhouse. $$-$$$$

The Saloon, 14. 200 E Chestnut St
☎ 280-5454. Steakhouse. $$-$$$$

!Salpicòn! 4. 1252 N Wells St
☎ 988-7811. Mexican. $$-$$$

Savannah's, 65. 1156 W Grand Ave
☎ 666-9944. Southern. $$-$$$

Scoozi! 77. 410 W Huron St
☎ 943-5900. Italian. $$

Seasons, 11. 120 E Delaware Pl
☎ 280-8800. New American.
$$$-$$$$

**Shaw's Crab House and Blue Crab
Lounge, 43.** 21 E Hubbard St
☎ 527-2722. Seafood. $$$-$$$$

Signature Room at the 95th, 16.
875 N Michigan Ave ☎ 787-9596.
American. $$$-$$$$

Spago, 50. 520 N Dearborn St
☎ 527-3700. Californian. $$$

Spiagga, 10. 980 N Michigan Ave
☎ 280-2750. Italian. $$$-$$$$

Spruce, 31. 238 E Ontario
☎ 642-3757. New American. $$$

Trattoria Parma, 55. 400 N Clark St
☎ 245-9933. Italian. $$-$$$

Topolobampo, 54. 445 N Clark St
☎ 661-1434. Mexican. $-$$$

Tsunami, 5. 1160 N Dearborn Ave
☎ 642-9911. Japanese. $$-$$$$

Tucci Milan, 46. 6 W Hubbard St
☎ 222-0044. Italian. $$

Wildfire, 72. 159 W Erie St
☎ 787-9000. American. $$-$$$

Wishbone, 66. 1800 W Grand Ave
☎ 829-3597. Southern. $$

Woo Lae Oak, 47. 30 W Hubbard St
☎ 645-0051. Korean. $-$$

Zinfandel, 51. 59 W Grand St
☎ 527-1818. New American. $$-$$$

$$$$ = over $50 $$$ = $30-$50 $$ = $20-$30 $ = under $20
Based on cost per person, excluding drinks, service, and 8.75% sales tax.

Loyola U
6400N

Devon Ave.

WEST
ROGERS PARK

Granville Ave.

ROGERS
PARK

Granville Ave.

North Shore Channel

Hollywood Park

Central Park Ave.

NORTH
PARK

Peterson Ave.

6000N

Lincoln Ave.

Bryn Mawr Ave.

Ashland Ave.

EDGEWATER

5600N

Rosehill
Cemetery

Bryn Mawr Ave.

Balmoral Ave.

Broadway

Sheridan Ave.

Balmoral Ave.

Bowmanville Ave.

Damen Ave.

Foster Ave.

5200N

Winnemac
Park

Leavitt St.

Argyle St.

St. Boniface
Cemetery

West
River
Park

East
River
Park

ALBANY
PARK

Kedzie Ave.

Virginia Ave.

Lawrence Ave.

4800N

RAVENS-
WOOD

Clark St.

UPTOWN

Wilson Ave.

Broadway

Wilson Ave.

Manor Ave.

Montrose Ave.

Welles
Park

Lincoln Ave.

Montrose Ave.

Graceland
Cemetery

Sheridan Ave.

Kimball Ave.

IRVING
PARK

Berteau Ave.

Horner
Park

2800W

2400W

2000W

Berteau Ave.

1600W

Central Park Ave.

Kedzie Ave.

Sacramento Ave.

California Ave.

Irving Park Rd.

4000N

NORTH
CENTER

Grace St.

1200W

Wrigley
Field

Grace St.

Addison St.

3600N

Damen Ave.

Western Ave.

Roscoe Ave.

LAKEVIEW

AVONDALE

Hamlin
Park

3200N

Ashland Ave.

Racine Ave.

Belmont Ave.

Elston Ave.

Wellington Ave.

LOGAN
SQUARE

N. Branch Chicago R.

2800N

Diversey Ave.

Lincoln Ave.

Logan
Sq.

Fullerton Ave.

Palmer
Sq.

Palmer St.

Rockwell St.

Milwaukee Ave.

2400N

Fullerton Ave.

DePaul U

DEPAUL

Clybourn Ave.

Racine Ave.

Humboldt Blvd.

BUCK-
TOWN

Armitage Ave.

Cortland St.

Leavitt St.

Damen Ave.

2000N

3200W

2800W

2400W

Wabansia Ave.

Western Ave.

Rockwell St.

1600N

Homan Ave.

Kedzie Ave.

Humboldt
Park

North Ave.

Hirsch St.

Wicker
Park

WEST
TOWN

2000

Division St.

1200N

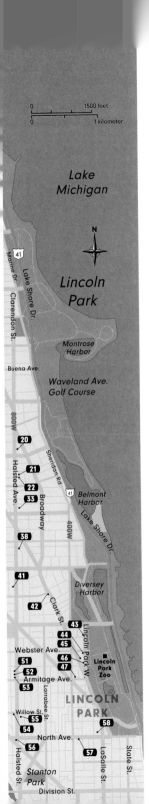

Listed by Site Number

NORTH SIDE

1 Heartland Café
2 Don Juan's
3 Viceroy of India
4 Udupi Palace
5 Via Veneto
6 Pasteur
7 Tomboy
8 Dellwood Pickle
9 Andies
10 Mei Shung
10 Spiagga
11 Ann Sather
12 La Donna
13 Julie Mai's Le Bistro
14 Bando
15 La Bocca della Verità
16 Arun's
17 Schulien's
18 Deleece
19 Strega Nona
20 Rhumba
21 Arco de Cuchilleros
22 Madam B
23 The Outpost
24 The Pepper Lounge
25 Matsuya
26 Jezebel
27 Addis Abeba
28 Bistrot Zinc
29 Brett's
30 Penny's Noodle Shop
31 Thai Classic
32 Mia Francesca
33 Yoshi's Café
34 Mama Desta's Red Sea
35 Ann Sather
36 Lutnia
37 Zum Deutschen Eck
38 Erwin
39 Penny's Noodle Shop
40 Kyoto
41 Raj Darbar
42 Clark Street Bistro
43 Ambria
43 Un Gran Café

44 Toulouse on the Park
45 Chicago Pizza & Oven Grinder Co.
46 Via Emilia
47 Geja's Café
48 Green Dolphin Street
49 Dee's
50 Sai Café
51 Relish
52 Café Ba-Ba-Reeba!
53 Charlie Trotter's
54 Vinci
55 Blue Mesa
56 Golden Ox
57 Flat Top Grill
58 Un DiAmo

BUCKTOWN & WICKER PARK

59 Frida's
60 Meritage
61 Merlot Joe
62 Rinconcito Sudamericano
63 Le Bouchon
64 Café Matou
65 Jane's
66 Club Lucky
67 Hi Ricky
68 Starfish
69 Feast
70 Café Med
71 Café Absinthe
72 Confusion
73 Soul Kitchen
74 Busy Bee
75 Luna Blu
76 Deluxe Diner
77 Bomgo Room
78 Twilight
79 Restaurant Okno

Listed Alphabetically

NORTH SIDE

Addis Abeba, 27. 3521 N Clark St ☎ 773/929-9383. Ethiopian. $

Ambria, 43. 2300 N Lincoln Park W ☎ 773/472-5959. French. $$$-$$$$

Andies, 9. 5253 N Clark St ☎ 773/784-8616. Lebanese. $

Ann Sather, 11. 5207 N Clark St ☎ 773/271-6677. Swedish/Breakfast $

Ann Sather, 35. 929 W Belmont Ave ☎ 773/348-2378. Swedish/Breakfast $

Arco de Cuchilleros, 21. 3445 N Halsted St ☎ 773/296-6046. Tapas. $

Arun's, 16. 4156 N Kedzie Ave ☎ 773/539-1909. Thai. $$-$$$

Bando, 14. 2200 W Lawrence Ave ☎ 773/728-7400. Korean. $$

Bistrot Zinc, 28. 3443 N Southport Ave ☎ 773/281-3443. French. $$-$$$

Blue Mesa, 55. 1729 N Halsted St ☎ 944-5990. Southwestern. $$

Brett's, 29. 2011 W Roscoe St ☎ 773/248-0999. Eclectic. $$-$$$

Café Ba-Ba-Reeba!, 52. 2024 N Halsted St ☎ 773/935-5000. Tapas. $$

Charlie Trotter's, 53. 816 W Armitage Ave ☎ 773/248-6228. New American. $$$$

Chicago Pizza & Oven Grinder Co., 45. 2121 N Clark St ☎ 773/248-2570. Pizza. $

Clark Street Bistro, 42. 2600 N Clark St ☎ 773/525-9992. Mediterranean. $$-$$$

Dee's, 49. 1114 W Armitage Ave ☎ 773/477-1500. Chinese. $$

Deleece, 18. 4004 N Southport Ave ☎ 773/325-1710. Eclectic. $$

Dellwood Pickle, 8. 1475 W Balmoral Ave ☎ 773/271-7728. American. $-$$

Don Juan's, 2. 6730 Northwest Hwy ☎ 773/775-6438. Mexican. $$-$$$

Erwin, 38. 2925 N Halsted ☎ 773/528-7200. American. $$-$$$

Flat Top Grill, 57. 319 W North Ave ☎ 787-7676. Stir Fry. $

Geja's Café, 47. 340 W Armitage Ave ☎ 773/281-9101. Fondue. $$$

Golden Ox, 56. 1578 N Clybourn Ave ☎ 644-0780. German. $$-$$$

Green Dolphin Street, 48. 2200 N Ashland Ave ☎ 395-0066. American/International. $$$

Heartland Cafe, 1. 7000 N Glenwood Ave ☎ 773/465-8005. American/Vegetarian. $

Jezebel, 26. 3517 N Clark St ☎ 773/929-4000. Mediterranean. $$-$$$$

Julie Mai's Le Bistro, 13. 5025 N Clark St ☎ 773/784-6000. Vietnamese/French.$$-$$$

Kyoto, 40. 2534 N Lincoln Ave ☎ 773/477-2788. Japanese. $$

La Bocca della Verità, 15. 4618 N Lincoln Ave ☎ 773/784-6222. Italian. $$

La Donna, 12. 5146 N Clark St ☎ 773/561-9400. Italian. $$-$$$

Lutnia, 36. 5532 W Belmont Ave ☎ 773/282-5335. Polish. $$-$$$

Madam B, 22. 3441 N Halsted St ☎ 773/248-4040. Pan-Asian. $$

Mama Desta's Red Sea, 34. 3216 N Clark St ☎ 773/935-7561. Ethiopian. $

Matsuya, 25. 3469 N Clark St ☎ 773/248-2677. Japanese. $$

Mei Shung, 10. 5211 N Broadway ☎ 773/728-5778. Chinese. $$

Mia Francesca, 32. 3311 N Clark St ☎ 773/281-3310. Italian. $$-$$$

The Outpost, 23. 3438 N Clark St ☎ 773/244-1166. New American. $$

Pasteur, 6. 5525 N Broadway ☎ 773/878-1061. Vietnamese. $$-$$$

Penny's Noodle Shop, 30. 3400 N Sheffield Ave ☎ 773/281-8222. Pan-Asian. $

Penny's Noodle Shop, 39. 950 W Diversey Pkwy ☎ 773/281-8448. Pan-Asian. $

The Pepper Lounge, 24. 3441 N Sheffield Ave ☎ 773/665-7377. New American. $$

$$$$ = over $50 $$$ = $30-$50 $$ = $20-$30 $ = under $20
Based on cost per person, excluding drinks, service, and 8.75% sales tax.

Raj Darbar, 41. 2660 N Halsted St
☎ 773/348-1010. Indian. $-$$

Relish, 51. 2044 N Halsted St
☎ 773/868-9034. American. $$

Rhumba, 20. 3631 N Halsted St
☎ 773/975-2345. Brazilian. $$-$$$

Sai Café, 50. 2010 N Sheffield Ave
☎ 773/472-8080. Japanese. $$

Schulien's, 17.
2100 W Irving Park Rd
☎ 773/478-2100.
German-American. $$

Strega Nona, 19.
3747 N Southport Ave
☎ 773/244-0990. Italian. $$

Thai Classic, 31. 3332 N Clark St
☎ 773/404-2000. Thai. $-$$$

Tomboy, 7. 5402 N Clark St
☎ 773/907-0636. American. $$

Toulouse on the Park, 44.
2140 N Lincoln Park W
☎ 773/665-9071. French. $$$

Udupi Palace, 4.
2543 W Devon Ave ☎ 773/338-2152.
Indian/Vegetarian. $

Un DiAmo, 58. 1617 N Wells St
☎ 337-8881. Italian. $$

Un Gran Café, 43.
2300 N Lincoln Park W
☎ 773/348-8886. French. $$-$$$

Via Emilia, 46. 2119 N Clark St
☎ 773/248-6283. Italian. $$-$$$

Via Veneto, 5. 3449 W Peterson Ave
☎ 773/267-0888. Italian. $$

Viceroy of India, 3.
2520 W Devon Ave ☎ 773/743-4100.
Indian. $-$$

Vinci, 54. 1732 N Halsted St
☎ 266-1199. Italian. $$-$$$

Yoshi's Café, 33. 3257 N Halsted St
☎ 773/248-6160. French. $-$$$

Zum Deutschen Eck, 37.
2924 N Southport Ave
☎ 773/525-8390. German. $$

BUCKTOWN & WICKER PARK

Bongo Room, 77.
1470 W Milwaukee Ave
☎ 773/489-0690. Breakfast/Lunch. $

Busy Bee, 74. 1546 N Damen Ave
☎ 773/772-4433. Polish/Diner. $

Café Absinthe, 71.
1954 W North Ave ☎ 773/278-4488.
New American. $$-$$$

Café Matou, 64.
1846 N Milwaukee Ave
☎ 773/384-8911. Bistro. $$

Café Med, 70.
1950 W North Ave ☎ 773/278-3800.
Italian/Mediterranean. $$

Club Lucky, 66. 1824 W Wabansia
☎ 773/227-2300. Italian. $$

Confusion, 72. 1616 N Damen Ave
☎ 773/772-7100. Eclectic. $$-$$$

Deluxe Diner, 76.
1575 N Milwaukee Ave
☎ 773/342-6667. American. $-$$

Feast, 69. 1835 W North Ave
☎ 773/235-6361. Eclectic. $$

Frida's, 59. 2134 N Damen
☎ 773/337-4327. Mexican. $$

Hi Ricky, 67. 1852 W North Ave
☎ 773/276-8300. Pan-Asian. $-$$

Jane's, 65. 1655 W Cortland Ave
☎ 773/862-JANE.
American/Vegetarian. $$

Le Bouchon, 63. 1958 N Damen Ave
☎ 773/862-6600. Bistro. $$

Luna Blu, 75. 1554 N Milwaukee Ave
☎ 773/862-2600. Italian. $$

Meritage, 60.
2118 N Damen Ave ☎ 773/235-6434.
Pacific Northwest. $$

Merlot Joe, 61. 2119 N Damen Ave
☎ 773/252-5141. French. $$

Restaurant Okno, 79.
1332 N Milwaukee Ave
☎ 773/395-1313. Fusion. $$

Rinconcito Sudamericano, 62.
1954 W Armitage Ave
☎ 773/489-3126. Peruvian. $

Soul Kitchen, 73.
1576 N Milwaukee Ave
☎ 773/342-9742. Southern. $$

Starfish, 68. 1856 W North Ave
☎ 773/395-3474. Seafood. $$-$$$

Twilight, 78. 1924 W Division St
☎ 862-8757. Eclectic. $

Listed by Site Number

1	Nuevo Leon	7	House of Fortune	12	Lulu's
2	Playa Azul	8	August Moon	13	Army & Lou's
3	Phoenix	9	Gladys Luncheonette	14	Soul Queen
4	Hong Min	10	Original Pancake House	15	The Retreat
5	Emperor's Choice	11	Dixie Kitchen & Bait Shop		
6	Three Happiness				

Listed Alphabetically

August Moon, 8. 225 W 26th St
☎ 842-2951. Indonesian. $-$$$

Army & Lou's, 13. 420 E 75th St
☎ 773/483-3100. Soul Food. $-$$$

Dixie Kitchen & Bait Shop, 11.
5225 S Harper Ave ☎ 773/363-4943.
Cajun. $$

Emperor's Choice, 5.
2238 S Wentworth Ave ☎ 225-8800.
Chinese. $-$$$

Gladys Luncheonette, 9.
4527 S Indiana Ave ☎ 773/548-4566.
Soul Food. $

Hong Min, 4. 221 Cermak Rd.
☎ 842-5026. Chinese. $-$$

House of Fortune, 7.
2407 S Wentworth Ave ☎ 225-8800.
Chinese. $-$$$

Lulu's, 12. 1333 E 57th St
☎ 773/288-2988. Pan-Asian. $

Nuevo Leon, 1. 1515 W 18th St
☎ 421-1517. Mexican. $-$$

Original Pancake House, 10.
1517 E Hyde Park Blvd
☎ 773/288-2322. Breakfast. $

Phoenix, 3. 2131 S Archer Ave
☎ 328-0848. Chinese. $-$$$

Playa Azul, 2. 1514 W 18th St
☎ 421-2552. Mexican. $-$$

The Retreat, 15. 605 E 111th St
☎ 773/568-6000. Southern. $$

Soul Queen, 14. 9031 S Stony Island
Ave ☎ 773/731-3366. Southern. $

Three Happiness, 6.
2130 S Wentworth Ave ☎ 791-1229.
Chinese/Dim Sum. $

$$$$ = over $50 $$$ = $30–$50 $$ = $20–$30 $ = under $20
Based on cost per person, excluding drinks, service, and 8.75% sales tax.

Listed by Site Number

1 Clarion Quality Inn at O'Hare

2 Ramada Plaza Hotel O'Hare

3 Best Western at O'Hare

4 O'Hare Marriott

5 Sheraton Gateway Suites

6 Westin Hotel O'Hare

7 Marriott Suites

8 Hyatt Regency O'Hare

9 Hotel Sofitel

10 Rosemont Suites Hotel

11 Holiday Inn O'Hare International

12 O'Hare Hilton

Listed Alphabetically

Best Western at O'Hare, 3. 10300 W. Higgins Rd, Rosemont ☎ 847/296-4471. ⊠ 847/296-4958. $$

Clarion Quality Inn at O'Hare, 1. 6810 N. Mannheim Rd, Rosemont ☎ 847/297-1234. ⊠ 847/297-5287. $-$$

Holiday Inn O'Hare International, 11. 5440 N. River Rd, Rosemont ☎ 847/671-6350. ⊠ 847/671-5406. $$$

Hotel Sofitel, 9. 5550 N. River Rd, Rosemont ☎ 847/678-4488. ⊠ 847/678-4244. $$$$

Hyatt Regency O'Hare, 8. 9300 W. Bryn Mawr Ave, Rosemont ☎ 847/696-1234. ⊠ 847/696-0139. $$$$

Marriott Suites, 7. 6155 N. River Rd, Rosemont ☎ 847/696-4400. ⊠ 847/696-2112. $$-$$$

O'Hare Hilton, 12. O'Hare International Airport ☎ 773/686-8000. ⊠ 773/601-2339. $$-$$$$

O'Hare Marriott, 4. 8535 W. Higgins Rd ☎ 773/693-4444. ⊠ 773/714-4296. $-$$$

Ramada Plaza Hotel O'Hare, 2. 6600 N. Mannheim Rd, Rosemont ☎ 847/827-5131. ⊠ 847/827-5659. $-$$

Rosemont Suites Hotel, 10. 5500 N. River Rd, Rosemont ☎ 847/678-4000. ⊠ 847/928-7659. $$$

Sheraton Gateway Suites, 5. 6501 N. Mannheim Rd, Rosemont ☎ 847/699-6300. ⊠ 847/699-0391. $$$-$$$$

Westin Hotel O'Hare, 6. 6100 N. River Rd, Rosemont ☎ 847/698-6000. ⊠ 847/698-3522. $$-$$$$

$$$$ = over $175 $$$ = $120–$175 $$ = $80–$120 $ = under $80

All prices are for a standard double room, excluding 14.9% room tax.

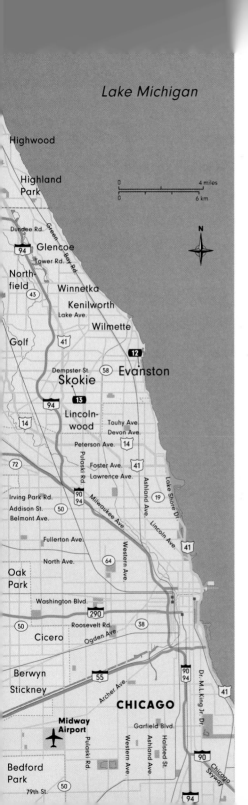

Lake Michigan

Highwood

Highland Park

Dundee Rd.

94 Glencoe

Tower Rd.

North-field 43

Winnetka

Kenilworth

Lake Ave.

Golf 41

Wilmette

Dempster St. 58

Skokie

Evanston 12

94 13

Lincoln-wood

Touhy Ave.

Devon Ave.

Peterson Ave. 14

72

Foster Ave. 41

Lawrence Ave.

Irving Park Rd.

Addison St. 50

Belmont Ave.

90 94

Fullerton Ave.

North Ave. 64

Oak Park

Washington Blvd.

290

50

Roosevelt Rd. 38

Cicero

Ogden Ave.

Berwyn

55

Stickney

Archer Ave.

90 94

41

CHICAGO

Midway Airport

Garfield Blvd.

Bedford Park

50

79th St.

90

94

0 ⸻ 4 miles
0 ⸻ 6 km

N

Listed by Site Number

1 Marriott's Lincolnshire Resort
2 Marriott Suites
3 Hyatt
4 Embassy Suites
5 Northbrook Hilton
6 Sheraton-North Shore
7 Amerisuites
8 Marriott-Schaumburg
9 Hyatt Regency Woodfield
10 Wyndham Garden-Schaumburg
11 Doubletree Guest Suites-Glenview
12 Omni Orrington
13 North Shore Doubletree
14 Courtyard Elmhurst
15 Embassy Suites
16 Hilton Suites
17 Wyndham Garden
18 Radisson
19 Hilton
20 Hyatt
21 Courtyard-Naperville
22 Holiday Inn Select
23 Doubletree-Downers Grove
24 Marriott Suites
25 Willowbrook Holiday Inn
26 Renaissance Oak Brook
27 Hyatt Regency
28 Oak Brook Hills
29 LaGrange Countryside Holiday Inn

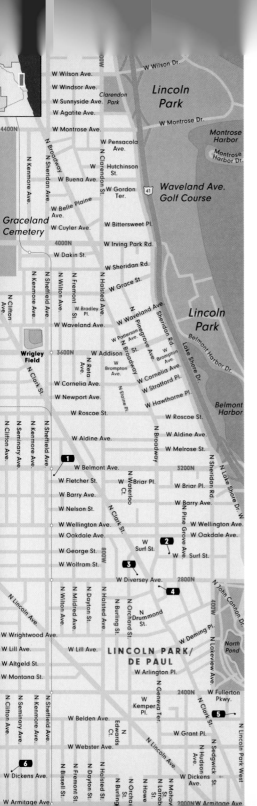

Listed by
Site Number

NORTH SIDE

1 City Suites Hotel
2 Surf Hotel
3 Days Inn Lincoln Park North
4 Comfort Inn of Lincoln Park
5 Belden-Stratford
6 City Scene & Breakfast

DOWNTOWN & NEAR NORTH

7 Omni Ambassador East
8 Ambassador West
9 Claridge Hotel
10 Sutton Place Hotel
11 Talbott
12 Whitehall Hotel
13 Four Seasons
14 The Drake
15 Westin Michigan Avenue
16 Regal Knickerbocker Hotel
17 Doubletree Guest Suites
18 Tremont
19 Raphael Chicago
20 Seneca
21 Ritz-Carlton
22 Summerfield Suites Hotel
23 HoJo Inn
24 River North Hotel
25 Embassy Suites
26 Cass Hotel
27 Omni Chicago Hotel
28 Holiday Inn Chicago City Centre
29 Best Western Inn of Chicago
30 Lenox Suites
31 Chicago Marriott Downtown
32 Hotel Inter-Continental Chicago
33 Sheraton Chicago Hotel and Towers
34 Courtyard by Marriott Chicago Downtown

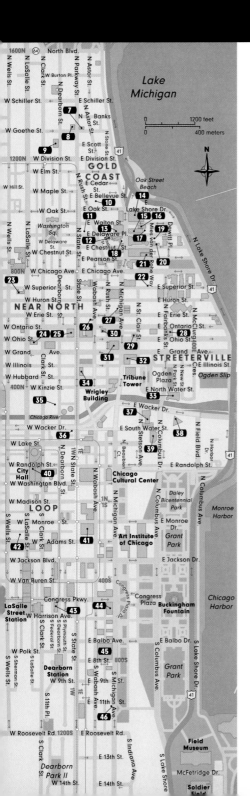

Listed by Site Number (cont.)

35 Westin River North

36 Renaissance Chicago Hotel

37 Hyatt Regency

38 Swissôtel

39 Fairmont

40 Hotel Allegro Chicago

41 Palmer House Hilton

42 Midland Hotel

43 Hyatt on Printers Row

44 Ramada Congress

45 Chicago Hilton and Towers

46 Best Western Grant Park Hotel

Listed Alphabetically

GREATER CHICAGO

Amerisuites, 7. 2111 S Arlington Heights Rd, Arlington Heights ☎ 847/956-1400. 🖷 847/956-0804. $$

Courtyard-Elmhurst, 14. 370 N IL at IL 64, Elmhurst ☎ 630/941-9444. 🖷 630/941-3539. $

Courtyard-Naperville, 21. 1155 E Diehl Rd, Naperville ☎ 630/505-0550. 🖷 630/505-8337. $$-$$$

Doubletree-Downers Grove, 23. 2111 Butterfield Rd, Downers Grove ☎ 630/971-2000. 🖷 630/971-1021. $-$$

Doubletree Guest Suites-Glenview, 11. 1400 Milwaukee Ave, Glenview ☎ 847/803-9800. 🖷 847/803-8026. $$-$$$

Embassy Suites, 15. 707 E Butterfield Rd, Lombard ☎ 630/969-7500. 🖷 630/969-8776. $$$

Embassy Suites, 4. 1445 Lake Cook Rd, Deerfield ☎ 847/945-4500. 🖷 847/945-7795. $-$$

Hilton, 19. 3003 Corporate West Dr, Lisle ☎ 630/505-0900. 🖷 630/505-0479. $-$$

Hilton Suites, 16. 10 Drury Lane, Oakbrook Terrace ☎ 630/941-0100. 🖷 630/941-0487. $$-$$$

Holiday Inn Select, 22. 1801 N Napier Blvd, Naperville ☎ 630/505-4900. 🖷 30/505-8239. $

Hyatt, 20. 1400 Corporetum Dr, Lisle ☎ 630/852-1234. 🖷 630/852-1260. $$$

Hyatt, 3. 1750 Lake Cook Rd, Deerfield ☎ 847/945-3400. 🖷 847/945-3563. $-$$

Hyatt Regency, 27. 1909 Spring Rd, Oak Brook ☎ 630/573-1234. 🖷 630/573-1133. $-$$$

Hyatt Regency Woodfield, 9. 1800 E Golf Rd, Schaumburg ☎ 847/605-1234. 🖷 847/605-0328. $$-$$$

LaGrange Countryside Holiday Inn, 29. 6201 Joliet Rd, Countryside ☎ 708/354-4200. 🖷 708/354-4241. $$

Marriott-Schaumburg, 8. 50 N Martingale Rd, Schaumburg ☎ 847/240-0100. 🖷 847/240-2388. $-$$$

Marriott Suites, 2. 2 Parkway N, Deerfield ☎ 847/405-9666. 🖷 847/405-0354. $-$$

Marriott Suites, 24. 1500 Opus Place, Downers Grove ☎ 630/852-1500. 🖷 630/852-6527 $-$$

Marriott's Lincolnshire Resort, 1. 10 Marriott Drive, Lincolnshire ☎ 847/634-0100. 🖷 847/634-1278. $-$$

North Shore Doubletree, 13. 9599 Skokie Blvd, Skokie ☎ 847/679-7000. 🖷 847/679-9841. $$

Northbrook Hilton, 5. 2855 N Milwaukee Ave, Northbrook ☎ 847/480-7500. 🖷 847/480-0827. $$

Oak Brook Hills, 28. 3500 Midwest Rd, Oak Brook ☎ 630/850-5555. 🖷 630/850-5569. $-$$

Omni Orrington, 12. 1710 Orrington Ave, Evanston ☎ 847/866-8700. 🖷 847/866-8724. $$$

Radisson, 18. 3000 Warrenville Rd, Lisle ☎ 630/505-1000. 🖷 630/505-1165. $-$$$

Renaissance Oak Brook, 26. 2100 Spring Rd, Oak Brook ☎ 630/573-2800. 🖷 630/573-7134. $$-$$$

Sheraton-North Shore, 6. 933 Skokie Rd, Northbrook ☎ 847/498-6500. 🖷 847/498-9558. $$

Willowbrook Holiday Inn, 25. 7800 S Kingery Hwy, Willowbrook ☎ 630/325-6400. 🖷 630/325-2362. $

Wyndham Garden, 17. 17 W 350 22nd St, Oakbrook Terrace ☎ 630/833-3600. 🖷 630/833-7037. $-$$

Wyndham Garden-Schaumburg, 10. 800 National Pkwy, Schaumburg ☎ 847/605-9222. 🖷 847/605-9240. $-$$

NORTH SIDE, NEAR NORTH & DOWNTOWN

Ambassador West, 8. 1300 N State Pkwy ☎ 787-3700. 🖷 640-2967. $$$

Belden-Stratford, 5. 2300 N Lincoln Park W ☎ 773/281-2900. 🖷 773/880-2039. $$$

Best Western Grant Park Hotel, 46. 1100 S Michigan Ave ☎ 922-2900. 🖷 922-8812. $$

Best Western Inn of Chicago, 29. 162 E Ohio St ☎ 787-3100. 🖷 573-3136. $$$

Cass Hotel, 26. 640 N Wabash Ave ☎ 787-4030. 🖷 787-8544. $

Chicago Hilton and Towers, 45. 720 S Michigan Ave ☎ 922-4400. 🖷 922-5240. $$$

Chicago Marriott Downtown, 31.
540 N Michigan Ave ☎ 836-0100.
🖷 836-6139. $$$$

City Scene Bed & Breakfast, 6.
2101 N Clifton Ave ☎ 773/549-1743. $$

City Suites Hotel, 1. 933 W Belmont
☎ 773/404-3400. 🖷 773/404-3405. $

Claridge Hotel, 9. 1244 N Dearborn
Pkwy ☎ 787-4980. 🖷 266-0978. $$

Comfort Inn of Lincoln Park, 4.
601 W Diversey Pkwy
☎ 773/348-2810. 🖷 773/348-1912. $$

**Courtyard by Marriott Chicago
Downtown, 34.** 30 E Hubbard St
☎ 329-2500. 🖷 329-0293. $$$

Days Inn Lincoln Park North, 3.
644 W Diversey Pkwy
☎ 773/525-7010. 🖷 773/525-6998. $

Doubletree Guest Suites, 17.
198 E Delaware Place ☎ 664-1100.
🖷 664-9881

The Drake, 14. 140 E Walton Pl
☎ 787-2200. 🖷 787-1431. $$$$

Embassy Suites, 25. 600 N State St
☎ 943-3800. 🖷 943-7629. $$$$

Fairmont, 39. 200 N Columbus Dr
☎ 565-8000. 🖷 856-1032. $$$$

Four Seasons, 13. 120 E Delaware Pl
☎ 280-8800. 🖷 280-1748. $$$$

HoJo Inn, 23. 720 N LaSalle St
☎ 664-8100. 🖷 664-2356. $

**Holiday Inn Chicago City Centre,
28.** 300 E Ohio St ☎ 787-6100.
🖷 787-3055

Hotel Allegro Chicago, 40.
171 W Randolph St ☎ 236-0123.
🖷 236-3177. $$

**Hotel Inter-Continental Chicago,
32.** 505 N Michigan Ave ☎ 944-4100.
🖷 944-3050. $$$$

Hyatt on Printer's Row, 43.
500 S Dearborn St ☎ 986-1234.
🖷 939-2468. $$$

Hyatt Regency, 37. 151 E Wacker Dr
☎ 565-1234. 🖷 565-2966. $$$$

Lenox Suites, 30. 616 N Rush St
☎ 337-1000. 🖷 337-7217. $$

Midland Hotel, 42. 172 W Adams St
☎ 332-1200. 🖷 332-5909. $$$

Omni Ambassador East, 7.
1301 N State Pkwy ☎ 787-7200.
🖷 787-4760. $$$

Omni Chicago Hotel, 27.
676 N Michigan Ave
☎ 944-6664. 🖷 266-3015. $$$$

Palmer House Hilton, 41.
17 E Monroe St ☎ 726-7500.
🖷 263-2556. $$$$

Ramada Congress, 44.
520 S Michigan Ave ☎ 427-3800.
🖷 427-4280. $$

Raphael Chicago, 19.
201 E Delaware Pl ☎ 943-5000.
🖷 943-9483. $$$

Regal Knickerbocker Hotel, 16.
163 E Walton Pl ☎ 751-8100.
🖷 751-9205. $$$

Renaissance Chicago Hotel, 36.
1 W Wacker Dr ☎ 372-7200.
🖷 372-0093. $$$$

Ritz-Carlton, 21. 160 E Pearson St
☎ 266-1000. 🖷 266-1194. $$$$

River North Hotel, 24. 125 W Ohio St
☎ 467-0800. 🖷 467-1665. $$

Seneca, 20. 200 E Chestnut St
☎ 787-8900. 🖷 988-4438. $$$

**Sheraton Chicago Hotel and
Towers, 33.** 301 E North Water St
☎ 464-1000. 🖷 464-9140. $$$$

Summerfield Suites Hotel, 22.
166 E Superior St ☎ 787-6000.
🖷 787-4331. $$$$

Surf Hotel, 2. 555 W Surf St
☎ 773/528-8400. 🖷 773/528-8483. $

Sutton Place Hotel, 10. 21 E Bellevue
Pl ☎ 266-2100. 🖷 266-2141. $$$$

Swissôtel, 38. 323 E Wacker Dr
☎ 565-0565. 🖷 565-0540. $$$$

Talbott, 11. 20 E Delaware Pl
☎ 944-4970. 🖷 944-7241. $$$$

Tremont, 18. 100 E Chestnut St
☎ 751-1900. 🖷 751-8691. $$$$

Westin Michigan Avenue, 15.
909 N Michigan Ave ☎ 943-7200.
🖷 943-9347. $$$$

Westin River North, 35.
320 N Dearborn St ☎ 744-1900.
🖷 527-2650. $$$$

Whitehall Hotel, 12.
105 E Delaware Pl ☎ 944-6300.
🖷 944-8552. $$$$

$$$$ = over $175 $$$ = $120–$175 $$ = $80–$120 $ = under $80
All prices are for a standard double room, excluding 14.9% room tax.

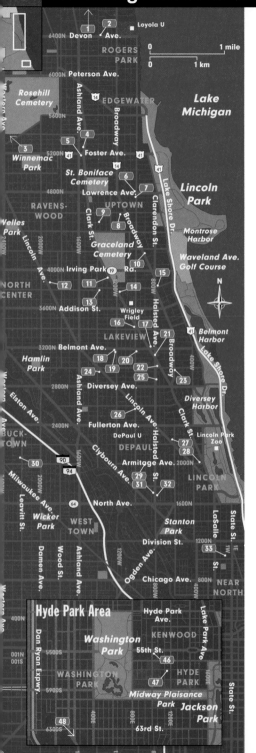

**Listed by
Site Number**

1 Lifeline Theater
2 Center Theater Ensemble
3 Ravinia Festival
4 Footsteps Theatre Company
5 Neo-Futurarium
6 Aragon Ballroom
7 Dance Center of Columbia College
8 Pegasus Players, O'Rourke Performing Arts Center
9 Black Ensemble Theater
10 Profiles Theatre
11 Live Bait Theater
12 American Theater Company
13 Mercury Theater
14 Annoyance Theatre
15 Strawdog Theatre Company
16 Stage Left Theatre
17 Voltaire Theatre
18 Bailiwick Repertory
19 Theatre Building
20 The Vic
21 Briar Street Theatre
22 Ivanhoe Theater
23 European Repertory Theatre
24 Athenaeum Theatre
24 Chicago Opera Theatre
25 Organic Touchstone Company
26 Apollo Theater
27 Victory Gardens Theater
28 Park West
29 Old Town School of Folk Music
30 Eclipse Theatre Company
31 Steppenwolf Theatre Company
32 Royal George Theatre
33 Shakespeare Repertory Theater
46 Court Theatre
47 Mandel Hall
48 ETA Creative Arts Foundation

Performing Arts/Downtown

MAP **54**

Listed by Site Number

34 Civic Opera House

35 Chicago Theatre

36 Chicago Cultural Center

37 Shubert Theatre

38 Goodman Theatre

39 Symphony Center

40 Auditorium Theatre

41 UIC Theater

42 Mayfair Theatre

43 DePaul University Merle Reskin Theatre

44 Getz Theater at Columbia College

Listed Alphabetically

American Theater Company, 12.
3855 N Lincoln Ave ☎ 773/929-1031

Annoyance Theatre, 14.
3747 N Clark St ☎ 773/929-6200

Apollo Theater, 26.
2540 N Lincoln Ave ☎ 773/935-6100

Aragon Ballroom, 6.
1106 W Lawrence Ave
☎ 773/561-9500

Arie Crown Theater, 45.
McCormick Place, 2301 S Lake Shore Dr ☎ 791-6190

Athenaeum Theatre, 24.
2936 N Southport Ave
☎ 773/935-6860

Auditorium Theatre, 40.
50 E Congress Pkwy ☎ 902-1500

Bailiwick Repertory, 18.
1229 W Belmont Ave ☎ 773/883-1090

Black Ensemble Theater, 9.
4520 N Beacon St ☎ 773/769-4451

Briar Street Theatre, 21.
3133 N Halsted St ☎ 773/348-4000

Center Theater Ensemble, 2.
1346 W Devon Ave ☎ 773/508-5422

Chicago Cultural Center, 36.
78 E Washington St ☎ 913-9446

Chicago Opera Theatre, 24. 2936 N Southport Ave ☎ 773/292-7578

Listed Alphabetically (cont.)

Chicago Theatre, 35.
175 N State St ☎ 902-1500

Civic Opera House, 34.
20 N Wacker Dr ☎ 419-0033

Court Theatre, 46.
5535 S Ellis Ave ☎ 773/753-4472

Dance Center of Columbia College, 7. 4730 N Sheridan Rd
☎ 773/989-3310

DePaul University Merle Reskin Theatre, 43. 60 E Balbo Dr
☎ 922-1999

Eclipse Theatre Company, 30.
2074 N Leavitt St ☎ 773/862-7415

ETA Creative Arts Foundation, 48.
7558 S South Chicago Ave
☎ 773/752-3955

European Repertory Theatre, 23.
615 W Wellington ☎ 773/248-0577

Footsteps Theatre Company, 4.
5230 N Clark St ☎ 773/878-4840

Getz Theater at Columbia College, 44. 72 E 11th St ☎ 663-1600, ext. 6126

Goodman Theatre, 38.
200 S Columbus Dr ☎ 443-3800

Ivanhoe Theater, 22.
750 W Wellington Ave ☎ 773/975-7171

Lifeline Theatre, 1.
6912 N Glenwood ☎ 773/761-4477

Live Bait Theater, 11.
3914 N Clark St ☎ 773/871-1212

Ivanhoe Theater, 22.
750 W Wellington Ave ☎ 773/975-7171

Lyric Opera of Chicago, 34.
20 N Wacker Dr ☎ 332-2244

Mayfair Theatre, 42.
636 S Michigan Ave ☎ 786-9120

Mercury Theater, 13.
3745 N Southport ☎ 773/325-1700

Neo-Futurarium, 5.
5153 N Ashland ☎ 773/275-5255

Old Town School of Folk Music, 29.
909 W Armitage ☎ 773/525-7793

Organic Touchstone Company, 25.
2851 N Halsted St ☎ 773/404-4700

Park West, 28.
322 W Armitage Ave ☎ 773/929-5959

Pegasus Players, O'Rourke Performing Arts Center, 8.
1145 W Wilson Ave ☎ 773/878-9761

Profiles Theatre, 10.
4147 N Broadway ☎ 773/549-1815

Ravinia Festival, 3.
Lake Cook & Green Bay Rds,
Highland Park ☎ 847/266-5100

Royal George Theatre, 32.
1641 N Halsted St ☎ 988-9000

Shakespeare Repertory Theater, 33. 1016 N Dearborn Pkwy
☎ 642-2273

Shubert Theatre, 37.
22 W Monroe St ☎ 902-1500

Stage Left Theatre, 16.
3408 N Sheffield ☎ 773/883-8830

Steppenwolf Theatre Company, 31.
1650 N Halsted St ☎ 335-1650

Strawdog Theatre Company, 15.
3829 N Broadway ☎ 773/528-9696

Symphony Center, 39.
220 S Michigan Ave ☎ 294-3000

Theatre Building, 19.
1225 W Belmont Ave ☎ 773/327-5252

UIC Theater, 41.
1044 W Harrison St ☎ 996-2939

The Vic, 20. 3145 N Sheffield Ave
☎ 773/929-5959.

Victory Gardens Theater, 27.
2257 N Lincoln Ave ☎ 773/871-3000

Voltaire Theatre, 17.
3231 N Clark Ave ☎ 773/528-3136

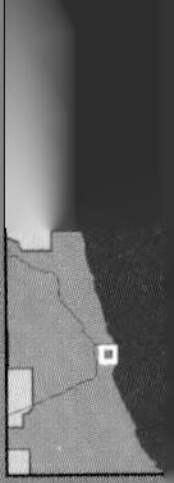

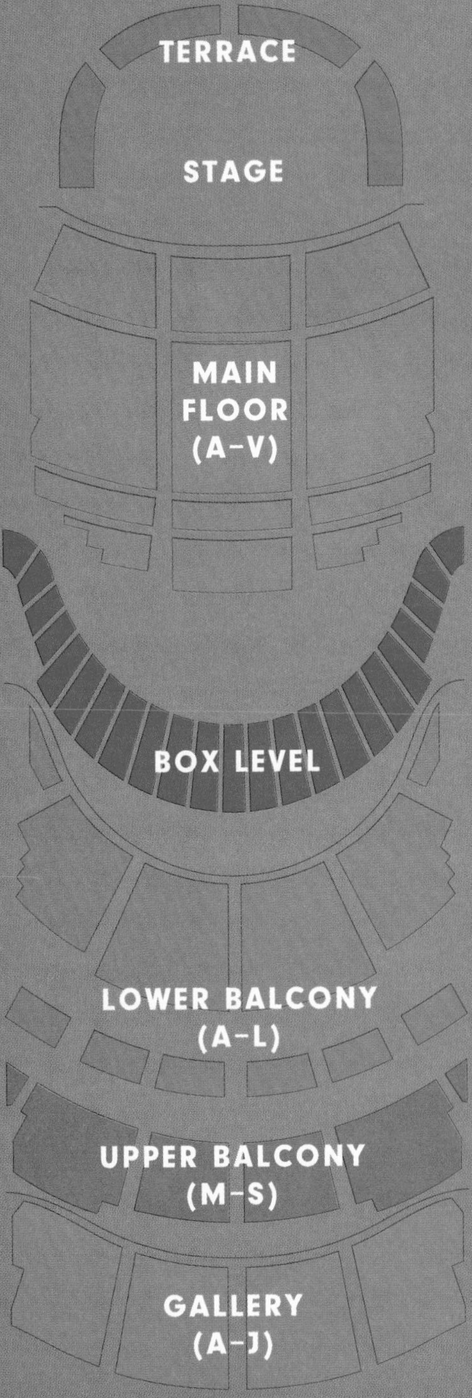

TERRACE

STAGE

MAIN
FLOOR
(A-V)

BOX LEVEL

LOWER BALCONY
(A-L)

UPPER BALCONY
(M-S)

GALLERY
(A-J)

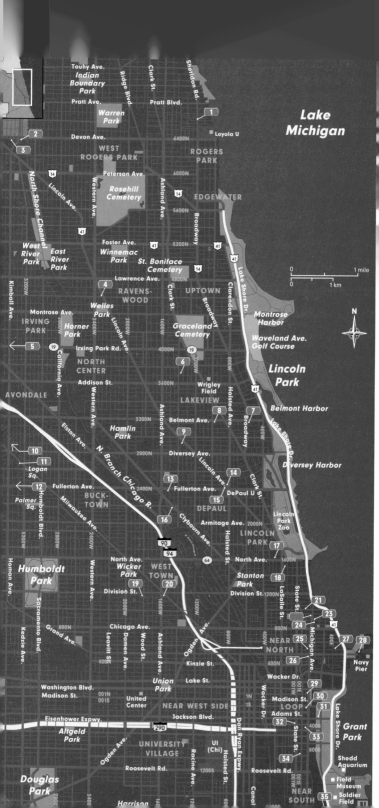

Listed by Site Number

1 Village North
2 Lincoln Village
3 Plaza
4 Davis
5 Patio
6 Music Box
7 Broadway
8 Vic Theatre
9 Kino-Eye Cinema at Xoinx Tearoom
10 Portage
11 Logan
12 Bricktown Square
13 Facets Multimedia
14 Biograph
15 Three Penny
16 Webster Place
17 Pipers Alley
18 Village
19 Celluloid Moviebar
20 Chicago Filmakers
21 Esquire
22 900 North Michigan
23 Instituo Cervantes
24 Water Tower Theater
25 600 N Michigan Ave
26 Instituto Italiano di Cultura
27 McClurg Court Cinemas
28 Navy Pier Imax
29 Chicago Cultural Ctr
30 School of the Art Institute
31 Film Center
32 Harold Washington Library Center
33 Fine Arts
34 Burnham Plaza
35 Hyde Park

Listed Alphabetically

Biograph Theatre, 14.
2433 N Lincoln Ave ☎ 773/348-4123

Bricktown Square, 12. 6420 W Fullerton Ave ☎ 773/622-6999

Broadway, 7.
3175 N Broadway ☎ 773/327-4114

Burnham Plaza, 34.
826 S Wabash Ave ☎ 922-1090

Celluloid Moviebar, 19.
1805 W Division St ☎ 707-8888

Chicago Cultural Center, 29.
78 E Washington St ☎ 346-3278

Chicago Filmakers, 20.
1545 W Division St ☎ 773/384-5533

Davis, 4.
4614 N Lincoln ☎ 773/784-0893

Esquire, 21. 58 E Oak St ☎ 280-0101

Facets Multimedia, 13.
1517 W Fullerton Ave ☎ 773/281-4114

Film Center, 31.
School of the Art Institute Columbus Dr and Jackson Blvd ☎ 443-3737

Fine Arts, 33.
418 S Michigan Ave ☎ 939-3700

Harold Washington Library Center, 32. 400 S State St ☎ 747-4050

Hyde Park, 35.
5238 S Harper Ave ☎ 773/288-4900

Instituto Cervantes, 23.
875 N Michigan Ave ☎ 335-1996

Instituto Italiano di Cultura, 26.
500 N Michigan Ave ☎ 822-9545

Kino-Eye Cinema at Xoinx Tearoom, 9. 2933 N Lincoln Ave ☎ 773/384-5533

Lincoln Village, 2. 6341 N McCormick St ☎ 773/604-4747

Logan, 11. 2646 N Milwaukee Ave ☎ 773/252-0627

McClurg Court Cinemas, 27.
330 E Ohio St ☎ 642-0723

Music Box, 6.
3733 N Southport ☎ 773/871-6604

Navy Pier Imax, 28.
700 E Grand ☎ 595-0090

900 North Michigan Cinemas, 22.
900 N Michigan Ave ☎ 787-1988

Patio, 5.
6008 W Irving Park ☎ 773/545-2006

Pipers Alley, 17.
1608 Wells St ☎ 642-7500

Plaza, 3.
3343 W Devon ☎ 773/539-3100

Portage, 10. 4050 N Milwaukee Ave ☎ 773/202-8000

School of the Art Institute, 30.
112 S Michigan Ave ☎ 345-3588

600 North Michigan Avenue, 25.
600 N Michigan Ave ☎ 255-9340

Three Penny, 15.
2424 N Lincoln Ave ☎ 773/935-5744

Vic Theatre, 8.
3145 N Sheffield ☎ 618-8439

Village, 18.
1548 N Clark ☎ 773/642-2403

Village North, 1.
6746 N Sheridan ☎ 773/764-9100

Water Tower Theater, 24.
845 N Michigan Ave ☎ 649-5790

Webster Place, 16.
1471 W Webster ☎ 773/327-3100

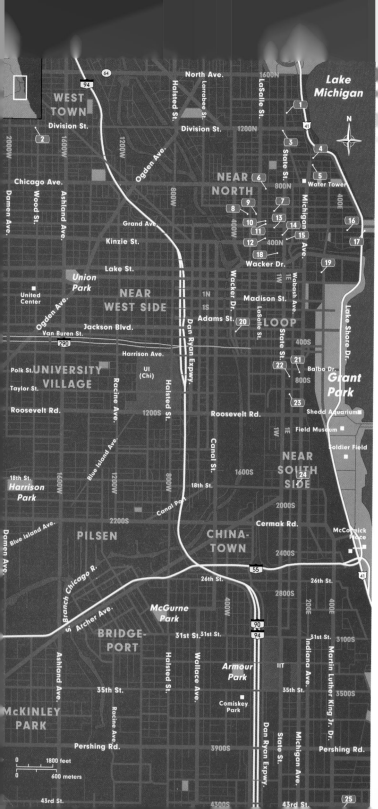

Listed by Site Number

1 Pump Room
2 Liquid Kitty
3 Yvette
4 Coq d'Or at the Drake
5 Seasons Lounge
6 Blue Chicago
7 Excalibur
8 Faces
9 Dennis Rodman's Illusions
10 Blue Chicago on Clark
11 Fadò Irish Pub
12 Baton Show Lounge
13 Jazz Showcase
14 Gentry
15 Andy's
16 Dick's Last Resort
17 Le Cabaret at Citè
18 House of Blues
19 Metropole Room
20 Yvette Wintergarden
21 Kitty O'Shea's
22 Buddy Guy's Legends
23 All Jokes Aside
24 Cotton Club
25 Checkerboard Lounge

Listed Alphabetically

All Jokes Aside, 23.
1000 S Wabash Ave ☎ 922-0577.
Comedy

Andy's, 15.
11 E Hubbard St ☎ 642-6805.
Jazz

Baton Show Lounge, 12.
436 N Clark St ☎ 644-5269.
Drag Club

Blue Chicago, 6.
736 N Clark St ☎ 642-6261. Blues

Blue Chicago on Clark, 10.
536 N Clark St ☎ 661-0100. Blues

Buddy Guy's Legends, 22.
754 S Wabash Ave ☎ 427-0333.
Blues

Checkerboard Lounge, 25.
423 E 43rd St ☎ 773/624-3240. Blues

Coq d'Or at the Drake, 4.
140 E Walton St ☎ 787-2200.
Piano Bar.

Cotton Club, 24.
1710 S Michigan Ave
☎ 341-9787. Jazz

Dennis Rodman's Illusions, 9.
157 W Ontario St ☎ 587-7792.
Dance Club

Dick's Last Resort, 16.
North Pier, 435 E. Illinois St
☎ 836-7870. Jazz

Excalibur, 7.
632 N Dearborn St
☎ 266-1944. Dance Club

Faces, 8.
223 W Ontario
☎ 440-3223

Fadò Irish Pub, 11.
100 W Grand Ave
☎ 836-0066. Irish

Gentry, 14.
440 N State St ☎ 664-1033.
Gay/Piano Bar

House of Blues, 18.
329 N Dearborn St
☎ 527-2583. Blues/Roots Music

Jazz Showcase, 13.
59 W Grand Ave
☎ 670-2473. Jazz

Kitty O'Shea's, 21.
720 S Michigan Ave
☎ 922-4400. Irish

Le Cabaret at Citè, 17.
505 N Lake Shore Dr
☎ 644-4050. Cabaret

Liquid Kitty, 2.
1807 W Division St
☎ 773/489-2700. DJ

Metropole Room, 19.
Fairmont Hotel, 200 N. Columbus Dr
☎ 565-8000. Jazz

Pump Room, 1.
1301 N State Pkwy ☎ 266-0360.
Piano Bar

Seasons Lounge, 5.
120 E Delaware Pl ☎ 280-8800.
Piano Bar

Yvette, 3. 1206 N State St
☎ 280-1700. Piano Bar

Yvette Wintergarden, 20.
311 S Wacker Dr ☎ 408-1242.
Piano Bar

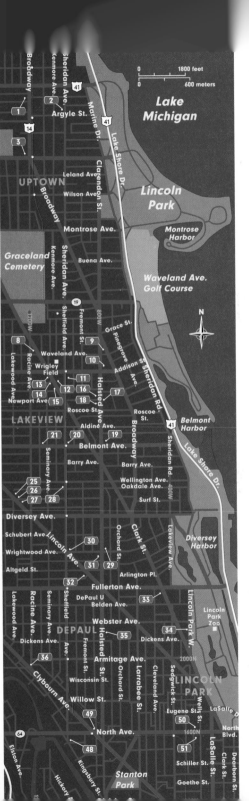

Listed by Site Number

1 Lakeview Lounge
2 Big Chicks
3 Green Mill
4 Augenblick
5 Así Es Columbia
6 Martyr's
7 Abbey Pub
8 Metro
8 Smart Bar
9 Charlies
10 Fusion
11 Hi-Tops Cafe
12 Improv Olympic
13 Cubby Bear
14 Sluggers
15 Wild Hare
16 Manhole
17 Side Trackz
18 Roscoe's
19 ComedySportz
20 Berlin
21 BLUES Etcetera
22 Schubas
23 Beat Kitchen
24 Tania's
25 Xoinx Tearoom
26 Thurston's
27 Elbo Room
28 Pops for Champagne
29 Girlbar
30 950 Club
31 Kingston Mines
32 Lounge Ax
33 Neo
34 Toulouse Cognac Bar
35 BLUES
36 Liquid
37 Convent
38 Green Dolphin St
39 Liar's Club
40 Rosa's
41 Tropicana d'Cache
42 Subterranean
43 Mad Bar
44 Red Dog
45 Double Door
46 The Note
47 Holiday Club
48 Crobar
49 Vinyl
50 Second City
51 Zanies

Listed Alphabetically

Abbey Pub, 7. 3420 W Grace St ☎ 773/478-4408. Irish Music

Asì Es Colombia, 5. 3910 N Lincoln Ave ☎ 773/348-7444. Latin/DJ

Augenblick, 4. 3907 N Damen ☎ 773/929-0994. DJ/Irish

Beat Kitchen, 23. 2100 W Belmont Ave ☎ 773/281-4444. Eclectic Live Music

Berlin, 20. 954 W Belmont Ave ☎ 773/348-4975. Dance Club

Big Chicks, 2. 5024 N Sheridan☎ 773/728-5511. Gay/Lesbian

BLUES, 35. 2159 N Halsted St ☎ 773/528-1012. Blues

BLUES Etcetera, 21. 1124 W Belmont Ave ☎ 773/525-8989. Blues

Charlie's, 9. 3726 N Broadway ☎ 773/871-8887. Gay/Country

ComedySportz, 19. 3209 N Halsted St ☎ 773/549-8080. Improv Comedy

Convent, 37. 1529 W Armitage Ave ☎ 773/395-8660. Dance Club

Crobar, 48. 1543 N Kingsbury ☎ 413-7000. Dance Club

Cubby Bear, 13. 1059 W Addison ☎ 773/327-1662. Rock

Double Door, 45. 1572 N Milwaukee Ave ☎ 773/489-3160. Rock

Elbo Room, 27. 2871 N Lincoln Ave ☎ 773/549-5549. Eclectic Live Music

Fusion, 10. 3631 N Halsted ☎ 773/975-6622. DJ/Gay

Girlbar, 29. 2625 N Halsted St ☎ 773/871-4210. Lesbian

Green Dolphin Street, 38. 2200 N Ashland Ave ☎ 773/395-0066. Jazz/Latin

Green Mill, 3. 4802 N Broadway ☎ 773/878-5522. Jazz

Hi-Tops Cafe, 11. 3551 N Sheffield Ave ☎ 773/348-0009. Sports Bar

Holiday Club, 47. 1417 N Milwaukee Ave ☎ 773/486-0686. DJ

Improv Olympic, 12. 3541 N Clark St ☎ 773/880-0199. Improv Comedy

Kingston Mines, 31. 2548 N Halsted St☎ 773/477-4646. Blues

The Lakeview Lounge, 1. 5110 N Broadway ☎ 773/769-0994. Country

Liar's Club, 39. 1665 W Fullerton Ave ☎ 773/665-1110. DJ

Liquid, 36. 1997 N Clybourn Ave ☎ 773/528-3400. Swing

Lounge Ax, 32. 2438 N Lincoln Ave ☎ 773/525-6620. Rock

Mad Bar, 43. 1640 N Damen Ave ☎ 773/227-2277. Nightclub

Manhole, 16. 3458 N Halsted St ☎ 773/975-9244. Gay

Martyr's, 6. 3855 N Lincoln Ave ☎ 773/404-9494. Eclectic Live Music

Metro, 8. 3730 N Clark St ☎ 773/549-0203. Rock

Neo, 33. 2350 N Clark St ☎ 773/528-2622. Dance Club

950 Club, 30. 950 W Wrightwood Ave ☎ 773/929-8955. Dance Club

The Note, 46. 1565 N Milwaukee Ave ☎ 773/489-0011. Jazz

Pops for Champagne, 28. 2934 N Sheffield Ave ☎ 773/472-1000. Jazz/Champagne Bar

Red Dog, 44. 1958 W North Ave ☎ 773/278-1009. Dance Club

Rosa's, 40. 3420 W Armitage Ave ☎ 773/342-0452. Blues

Roscoe's, 18. 3356 N Halsted St ☎ 773/281-3355. Gay/DJ

Schubas Tavern, 22. 3159 N Southport Ave ☎ 773/525-2508. Rock/Folk

Second City, 50. 1616 N Wells St ☎ 337-3992. Comedy

Side Trackz, 17. 3349 N Halsted St ☎ 773/477-9189. Gay/Lesbian/Video

Sluggers, 14. 3540 N Clark St ☎ 773/248-0055. Sports Bar

Smart Bar, 8. 3730 N Clark St ☎ 773/549-4140. Dance Club

Subterranean, 42. 2011 W North Ave ☎ 773/278-6600. Rock

Tania's, 24. 2659 N Milwaukee Ave☎ 773/235-7120. Salsa

Thurston's, 26. 1248 W George St ☎ 773/472-6900. Eclectic Live Music

Toulouse Cognac Bar, 34. 2140 N Lincoln Park West ☎ 773/665-9071. Cabaret

Tropicana d'Cache, 41. 2047 N Milwaukee Ave ☎ 773/489-9600. Latin

Vinyl, 49. 1615 N Clybourn Ave ☎ 587-8469. Nightclub

Wild Hare, 15. 3530 N Clark St ☎ 773/327-4273. Reggae/World Beat

Xoinx Tearoom, 25. 2933 N Lincoln Ave ☎ 773/665-1336. Coffeehouse

Zanies, 51. 1548 N Wells St ☎ 337-4027. Comedy

Notes